The Dance of Death

This translation is dedicated
to the memory of
John Gassner

August Strindberg

The Dance of Death

TRANSLATED BY ARVID PAULSON
WITH AN INTRODUCTION BY DANIEL SELTZER
AND PERFORMANCE NOTES BY ARVID PAULSON

W · W · NORTON & COMPANY

New York · London

W. W. Norton & Company, Inc., 500 Fifth Avenue, New York, N.Y. 10110
W. W. Norton & Company Ltd., 37 Great Russell Street, London WC1B 3NU

ISBN 0-393-00820-7

Printed in the United States of America

5 6 7 8 9 0

Contents

AUGUST STRINDBERG

August Strindberg was born in Stockholm on January 22, 1849. His early life was an unhappy one and so were the turbulent years that followed. Beset by poverty and continuously wrestling with his strange psyche, he nevertheless survived three disastrous marriages, and at his death on May 14, 1912, was mourned by the Swedish nation despite having been a thorn in its side throughout his remarkable literary career. Now acknowledged as one of the great geniuses of all times, he produced 55 volumes of plays, novels, short stories, essays, poems, scientific and historical works.

Introduction

Daniel Seltzer

THE ENDLESS WAR between men and women is the thematic concern which produced some of August Strindberg's most powerful stage narratives. In this "war," the opposing forces—the human needs of each sex—would become (in Strindberg's view, inevitably) forces of savage destruction. More, these destructive forces are shown to spring from what was identified, perhaps earlier in the lives of the warring characters, as highly energized attraction: love turned to hatred. Woven into such terms of conflict is Strindberg's belief that nurture itself—that defining characteristic of parents' love for their children, or of one love partner's attraction for the other—will eventually alter, and turn the need to give to the need to suffocate. These concerns, of course, related to the playwright's own life—and his remarkably neurotic need for and repulsion from women, both mistresses and wives, is amply documented, and he himself was agonizingly aware of the pattern in his behavior. This formula of struggle between a man and a woman, and the destructive actions it would produce, stands behind many of his scripts, and is the underlying theme of *The Dance of Death*. This subject matter had appeared early, for example, in *The Father* (1887), and then in *Miss Julie* (1888)—and indeed in other plays written long before *The Dance of Death*, which was composed in 1901. It was to be repeated the next year in *A Dream Play*, and again, five years later, in *The Ghost Sonata* and *The Pelican* (to mention only a few works in which this theme informs the action). No mode of action interested Strindberg more than this one, and he rang changes upon it throughout his career as a practicing playwright.

As in the other plays in which it occurs, this substantive material for plot contains potentially great theatrical energy, for by definition it evokes personalities which are alternatingly passive and active: the assault of one partner, in what Strindberg sees as the demonic duet of love and marriage, overpowers the other; then the energy changes, and sections of dialogue—indeed a whole play—may be seen as the sequence, in aggregate, of a pulsating rhythm of attack and response. Finally, resolution occurs in which one combatant is defeated, the other hardly victorious, but rather inwardly destroyed by his or her own violent hatred for the other. Strindberg often depicted the children of such a partnership—as in Part II of *The Dance of Death*—as striving somehow to survive such perverted nurture; but whether they do or not, their efforts form a continuation of the passive/active dynamic already established between their parents. This rhythm of assault and response in sexual terms had never before been so utilized by a playwright, although perhaps in the plays of the German, Frank Wedekind, more or less contemporary with Strindberg, a hint of the method had emerged; needless to say, this rhythm—soon to be made more accessible in the works of Freud (whose writings, by the way, there is no evidence that Strindberg had read)—would become stock-in-trade for many dramatists, beginning with Eugene O'Neill and currently manifested with a powerful consistency in the scripts of Harold Pinter.

It is important to examine the character relationships in *The Dance of Death* (particularly in Part I, which is frequently performed separately, since it stands as a full-length play), because their effects in this drama are typical not only of many earlier and later plays by Strindberg himself, but of manifestations of this dynamic in much other modern theatre.

In reading or performance, the major attribute of this action is an odd syncopation of energy and, simultaneously, a commensurately uneven ebb and flow of our feelings of connection with an individual character. For some pages—or minutes—of dialogue, the characters will seem to talk with each other (whatever their subject matter) in the diction of everyday life: answer follows question, motive produces an expectable response. During such exchange, we listen and feel "naturally"; nothing that is said or done actually surprises. Such stretches of dialogue are conventionally expository—they tell us where, and how, and why. During such exchanges of energy, "real" time is in control—that is, one minute of speech in the play is neither longer nor shorter than one minute in the world outside the theatre. Then, suddenly, abruptly, a change of rhythm will occur. Were this play a short poem, say, such a change might be compared to an almost grotesquely sudden alteration of metre. With no warning, a character will speak continuously for a long time, or fall to the floor in a fit, or aim her umbrella at another as one would a rifle; sounds and other stage effects—for example, the long and short buzzings of a telegraph receiver—can interrupt ongoing action in the same way. At such junctures, "real" time seems suspended. The result of these alterations of tempo is the syncopation mentioned above, and it is only natural to ask why they occur.

The logic of such explosions of energy—one might call them "chords" in the evolving texture of the play—is to be found not only in human behavior but in the ways Strindberg transmutes that behavior. So far, we have avoided those potentially troublesome terms, "naturalism" and "expressionism"; but if one is eventually to understand in simple terms what immense advances Strindberg made in the art of drama, this nomenclature must be used—though, I hope, with some new perception of its meaning. We are told in dictionaries of stage history that while it was the tendency of "naturalistic" playwrights to focus upon the external details of human behavior and environment, "expressionists" wanted rather to emphasize and define the inner world of motivation and action. So far, so good. The artists of the latter group would articulate, whatever their methods, what lies beyond immediate apprehension, and *express* the inner reality. In simple stage terms, then, what would normally be hidden in daily life would take on hard, physical manifestation—whether in the words of a person in a certain situation or the appearance of an object or a room.

In practical usage, it may be more meaningful to speak of an "Expressionist" playwright as *exposing* what is on the inside, whether of a human mind or a physical environment. It is a critical commonplace that Strindberg's career encompassed both naturalistic and expressionistic techniques; while he is known—rightly or not—as the father of "expressionism" in modern drama, he is equally famous for the preface written for *Miss Julie,* a manifesto of sorts for drama which deals with "natural" life. The dramatic techniques of *The Dance of Death* (and here one may speak with equal emphasis of Parts I and II) represent a fascinating combination of conventions dependent, first, on dialogue which seems to us "normal" in sequence and content, but which then apparently elicits these changes of rhythm and subject matter described above, and which, as the play unfolds before us, must seem—rightly—shockingly abrupt. These moments, as I have suggested, may be called "chords." As in an ongoing sequence of musical sounds, where potential harmonic changes are "stored up" and then released, as the composer, following rules of expectation and response, will change the key, so Strindberg—at very special junctures in the action—releases *accumulated* emotional energy, whether visually, verbally, or aurally.

When he does this, he is expressing what he has seen as the inner truth and reality of a behavioral phenomenon—in this case, as in so many others, the developing hatred among a husband, his wife, and another man of whom the husband has reason to be jealous. When, for example, Kurt observes of the Captain's and Alice's house, isolated both geographically and emotionally from the rest of the world, that there is poison in its very wallpaper, Strindberg is (obviously) eager for us to agree that what Kurt is talking about is the nature of the married relationship onstage. At just this moment, the Captain chokes and collapses on the floor. Why? Because Kurt's statement has so excited him as to cause a small stroke in response? Hardly. We never learn the "real" physiological cause for Edgar's fainting spells. When, in Chekhov's *The Sea Gull,* the old invalid Sorin feels faint and collapses after arguing with his sister about money, there is no question that the playwright intends to depict a very "natural" cause and response: Sorin is so worried and agitated that he becomes dizzy. The Captain in Strindberg's play, however, falls to the floor literally *because of the poison.* What is innerly real in the situation is exposed; the "expressionist" method opens up what would be normally hidden. Similarly, when Alice pounds out on the piano and the Captain dances to the savage theme song of the

x

play, "The March of the Boyars," he again faints: the music itself has come to represent simultaneously both his bullying assault on life itself and the tone of Alice's attacks upon him as well. When, as the action of the play moves forward, enough emotional response to the given situation has accumulated, an aggregate of movement or words—what we have called a chord—is signaled in the script. The almost grotesque placement of these moments has, as in "real" life, a causal connection to the facts; but this playwright is more interested in the innerly energized truth than with surface detail. For this reason, a play by Strindberg—and by that important line of dramatists influenced by him—expresses reality in what may seem at first to be obtuse effects interspersing apparently naturalistic dialogue. The effects—speeches, movements, whatever—are underpinned as often by a total emotional truth (in this case, a destructive battle between the sexes) as by detailed and individualized moments of motivation.

This does not mean that Strindberg's stage personalities are not deeply motivated by knowable psychological needs; quite the contrary. The selective expressionist mode, however, compresses these needs in such a way as to hold them, one might say, in suspension, over a period of acting time—and then releases them. When they are released, they cause commensurately powerful, and compressed, dramatic results. It is difficult to emphasize sufficiently the great effect this technique has had in the history of dramaturgy in the twentieth century. Beginning probably with Eugene O'Neill, every major playwright of the modern period has been in some manner influenced by Strindberg's conception of human behavior as it can be depicted onstage. The most important dramatists of the last few decades—Brecht, Genet, Ionesco, Miller, Albee, Williams, Pinter—all, in one way or another, reveal on examination a method of distributing event and reaction within the fabric of action which stems from Strindberg's syncopated variations of pace and rhythm. Indeed, perhaps Strindberg remains so profoundly modern specifically because he developed a technique which could probe the innermost recesses of human needs and conflicts, and then—suddenly and sometimes explosively—could *clarify* them, setting them forth onstage with such agonizing purity.

Performance Notes

Arvid Paulson

THE DANCE OF DEATH had its first performance at the end of September, 1905, at the Residenztheater in Cologne, Germany, and following its original première there, Parts I and II were given in forty cities.

In the fall of 1905 both parts were also given in Berlin, and in the fall of 1906 by Josef Jarno in Vienna. During the next two years the play was acted in Mannheim, Hamburg, Bremen and Berlin. In Riga it was presented in 1909.

The Swedish première took place at The Intimate Theatre (The Strindberg Theatre) in Stockholm on September 8, 1909, when Part I was given; and on October 1 Part II was presented. Strindberg instructed August Falck, who played the Captain, as follows: "First and last, the Captain must look old! His ugliness, age, and whiskey imbibing must show!" The critical reception after Part I was mixed, but after Part II less stinging. The play was given *en tour* in 1911.

In 1912 Max Reinhardt produced both parts at the Deutsches Theater in Berlin. Gertrud Eysoldt acted Alice and Paul Wegener the Captain's rôle. In 1915 Reinhardt brought the play to Sweden, where it was given at the Royal Theatre with Wegener and Rosa Bertens in the two leading rôles; and during the war it was given in Germany with tremendous success (1916).

In 1919 The Swedish Theatre presented the play with Tore Svennberg as the Captain and Pauline Brunius as Alice, touring with it 1920-23. In the fall of 1921 Part II was given at Malmö Theatre with Harriet Bosse in Judith's rôle.

The Royal Theatre gave Part II in the autumn of 1921. 1923 and 1924 Tore Svennberg again triumphed as the Captain opposite Hilda Borgström as Alice. 1926 it was given at the People's Theatre in Gothenburg, and the same year August Falck and

Manda Björling acted the play at the Civic Theatre in Helsingborg. 1934-37 Olof and Anna Hillberg played in it 423 times in the provinces.

In 1937 Poul Reumert of the Royal Danish Theatre gave guest appearances at the Royal Theatre in Stockholm in the rôle of the Captain, playing opposite Tora Teje. In the spring of 1938 it was produced at the Gothenburg Civic Theatre, and in the fall of that year the travelling government theatre presented the play in the provinces. In 1944 the Vasa Theatre in Stockholm produced it, and in 1949, the government theatre took it to various parts of Sweden. The same year, it was seen at the Blanche Theatre in Stockholm; and in the spring of 1952 Keve Hjelm staged the play at the Civic Theatre in Helsingborg. The Chamber Theatre in Stockholm gave Part II in the spring of 1954.

In 1954 the Halmstad Theatre was inaugurated with a performance acted by the Gothenburg Civic Theatre Company, and in the same year the Norrköping-Linköping Civic Theatre had its opening with the play, which later was acted by the ensemble in the provinces, and also in Denmark. In the fall of 1957 Sammy Friedman acted the Captain again at the Chamber Theatre, and in 1959 the Royal Theatre gave the play with Lars Hanson as the Captain. *The Dance of Death* was acted by the Royal Theatre Company *en tour* that same year, when it also appeared in Finland.

In 1928 the distinguished Poul Reumert of the Danish Royal Theatre was invited to appear in the play at the Odéon in Paris, where he proved his virtuosity by giving a flawless performance in superb French—a performance greatly admired by Antoine and Lugné Poe, who were among the audience.

The play has been given in practically every European country as well as in America, Mexico and South America. In England Robert Loraine gave a most successful performance of the play, although somewhat melodramatic, in the 1920's. It was also filmed in Italy, with Erich von Stroheim as the Captain. It has received extensive productions on radio in Sweden, Norway, Denmark, Latvia, Germany, Finland, Russia, Austria, France and in the U.S.A.

This play had its first performances in the U.S.A. by the Lister touring company, when Ethel Grey Terry acted Alice's rôle. In May of 1920 the newly formed Theatre Guild gave special performances of it at the Garrick Theatre, with Albert Parry playing the Captain's rôle and Helen Westley Alice's. 1935 the Federal Theatre gave the play for three weeks. In January, 1948, the play under the title The Last Dance was presented at the Belasco Theatre, Oscar Homolka playing the Captain and Jesse Royce Landis appearing in Alice's rôle, in which she gave a most brilliant performance—a performance that I doubt will ever be surpassed.

1966 Oscar Homolka again acted his excellent interpretation of Edgar, the Captain, at the Hampstead Theatre in London; and in Washington the Arena Theatre presented the play with Rip Torn and Viveca Lindfors in the leading rôles 1970. The play has also been seen at an off-Broadway theatre.

Perhaps the most brilliant production of recent years was that mounted by the National Theatre of Great Britain in 1967. Fortunately, the director, Glen Byam Shaw, respected the text (Parts I and II were given, with few cuts) and tone of the play, rather than imposing on it an alien shape. Squarely at the center was Sir Laurence Olivier as the Captain, in another of his heroic portrayals of antiheroes; he brought out the character's power and pettiness as well. Actors able to match Olivier at his best are not easily found, but Geraldine McEwen's beautiful, cold Alice and Robert Stephens' handsome, malleable Kurt fought him to a credible standoff. The production remained in the company's repertoire for three years and was recorded on film.

On April 28, 1971, this powerful drama was brought to the Ritz Theatre in New York in a mutilated version by Paul Avila Mayer. Acted by Rip Torn, Viveca Lindfors and Michael Strong it turned out to be a fiasco, lasting five nights. Another unsuccessful attempt was made by the American Shakespeare Festival Company at the Vivian Beaumont Theatre in 1974. The director, A. J.

Antoon, who had previously transplanted Shakespeare's *Much Ado about Nothing* to Teddy Roosevelt's America, had similarly Americanized Strindberg, both in his direction and in his adaptation of Strindberg's text (only Part I was given). Originally Max von Sydow and Joanne Woodward had been cast in the leading roles—a fascinating prospect—but on opening night the Captain was Robert Shaw, acting with bullish extroversion, and Alice was Zoe Caldwell, struggling against the disadvantages of an uncongenial and somewhat unfamiliar concept of her role (she had replaced Joanne Woodward late in rehearsals) and Antoon's grossly misconceived direction. This was hardly an adequate effort.

This chronicle suggests how far *The Dance of Death* has been adopted, if not quite assimilated, into the core repertoire of modern drama. The play makes extreme demands on the skill and stamina of its leading actors, and is full of traps for them and the director, but when responsibly directed and fearlessly acted in an authoritative translation it offers one of the cathartic dramatic experiences of our time.

Part One

Persons in Part I:

Edgar a captain in the fortress artillery.
Alice, his wife, formerly an actress.
Kurt, a quarantine master.
Jenny, a maid.
An Old Woman.
A Sentry. (Non-speaking rôle).

The Setting:

The interior of a round fortress tower of granite.

At the rear, a gateway with French windows, through which can be seen a seashore with battery emplacements, and the sea.

On either side of the entrance, a window with flower-boxes and birds in cages.

To the left of the entrance, an upright piano; further down-stage a sewing table and two reclining chairs.

On the right, half-way downstage, a writing table on which is placed a telegraph apparatus, and closer downstage stands a whatnot with framed portraits. Nearby is a *chaise-longue* or a sofa, sufficiently ample to be used for sleeping. A buffet (or a cabinet) stands against the wall. A hanging lamp is suspended from the ceiling.

On the wall, against which the piano is placed, hang two large laurel wreaths, with ribbons attached; they flank the framed portrait of a woman in a stage costume.

7

A hat- and coat-tree with army equipment, sabres, etc., stands near the rear doors, and close by is a bureau-desk.

To the right of the doorway hangs a mercury barometer.

On each side of the room there is a door, the one on the left leading to the kitchen and the one on the right leading to other rooms, as well as outside.

ACT I   SCENE 1

A mild autumn evening. At the back of the tower room, the French windows stand open, and in the background outside—down by the coastal battery emplacement—can be seen an artilleryman with his plumed helmet, on sentry duty. From time to time his sabre reflects the crimson rays of the setting sun. The sea lies dark and calm.

The Captain is seated in the armchair on the right of the sewing table, fingering an unlit cigar. He is in fatigue uniform, somewhat worn, and is wearing riding boots with spurs. He looks tired and bored.

Alice sits in the armchair on the left of the sewing table. Unoccupied with anything, she also looks tired, yet seems expectant.

THE CAPTAIN: Won't you play for me a little something?

ALICE: *(In an indifferent tone, without being snappish.)* What do you want me to play?

THE CAPTAIN: Whatever you feel like.

ALICE: But you don't like anything I do play.

THE CAPTAIN: And you don't like to play what I like.

ALICE: *(Evasively.)* Do you want the doors to be left open?

THE CAPTAIN: If you so wish.

ALICE: Let's leave them open, then. *(Silence.)* Why aren't you smoking?

THE CAPTAIN: Strong tobacco doesn't agree with me any more.

8

ALICE: *(Almost in a kindly tone.)* Smoke something milder, then—since you say smoking is your only joy.

THE CAPTAIN: Joy! What is joy—tell me that?

ALICE: Don't ask me. I know as little about it as you do. —Don't you want to have your whiskey now?

THE CAPTAIN: Not just yet.—What are we having for dinner?

ALICE: How should I know? Ask Kristin.

THE CAPTAIN: Isn't it time for mackerel soon? It's fall, isn't it?

ALICE: Yes—it's fall. . . .

THE CAPTAIN: Both outside and inside! But no matter! Apart from the cold that comes with autumn—inside and out—a grilled mackerel with a slice of lemon, and a glass of white burgundy, is not to be disdained.

ALICE: The thought of that promptly made you eloquent, didn't it?

THE CAPTAIN: Have we any burgundy left in the wine cellar?

ALICE: I didn't know that we have had a wine cellar for the past five years.

THE CAPTAIN: You don't seem to know anything. However, we *must* stock up for our silver wedding.

ALICE: Are you really serious about celebrating it?

THE CAPTAIN: Of course, I am.

ALICE: It would be more fitting for us to hide our misery—our twenty-five years of misery. . . .

THE CAPTAIN: We have had our miseries, Alice dear, but we have also had our moments of joy. . . . And we have to make use of the little time that is left—for after that comes the end.

ALICE: The end, you say? I only wish it were!

THE CAPTAIN: It *is* the end!—and all that is left of us could be put in a wheelbarrow and used to fertilize a garden plot.

ALICE: And all this ado for a garden plot. . . .

THE CAPTAIN: That is how it is, however. And it is not of my doing.

ALICE: All this fuss! *(Silence.)* Has the mail come?

THE CAPTAIN: Yes.

ALICE: Was the butcher's bill there?

9

THE CAPTAIN: Yes.

ALICE: How much was it?

THE CAPTAIN: (*Takes a sheet of paper from his pocket, puts on his spectacles, but takes them off immediately.*) You read what it says—I can't make it out.

ALICE: What's the matter with your eyes?

THE CAPTAIN: I don't know.

ALICE: Old age.

THE CAPTAIN: Nonsense! I?

ALICE: Yes, you—not I!

THE CAPTAIN: H'm.

ALICE: (*Taking a look at the bill.*) Will you be able to pay this?

THE CAPTAIN: Yes—but not immediately.

ALICE: Some time in the future, of course—after a year, when you have retired on a small pension and are unable to pay it. And later, when sickness sets in again. . . .

THE CAPTAIN: Sickness? I have never been sick—only a trifle indisposed—one single time, that's all. And I have twenty years yet to go.

ALICE: The doctor had a different opinion.

THE CAPTAIN: The doctor. . . .

ALICE: Yes, who else could give a trustworthy opinion?

THE CAPTAIN: I have no illness, and have never had any, nor shall I ever have any. When I die, I shall die all of a sudden —just drop dead—like an old soldier.

ALICE: Speaking of the doctor—you know that he is giving a party this evening.

THE CAPTAIN: (*Agitated.*) Well, what of it? We are not invited because we are not on intimate terms with him and his wife; and we are not intimate with them because we don't want to be—because I have contempt for both of them. They are riff-raff.

ALICE: You say that of everybody.

THE CAPTAIN: Because that's all everybody is—riff-raff.

ALICE: With one exception—you yourself.

THE CAPTAIN: Yes—for among all sorts of conditions of life I have invariably deported myself correctly and decently. That is why I do not belong in their category.

   (*Silence.*)

ALICE: Would you like to play a game of cards?

THE CAPTAIN: We may as well.

ALICE: (*Takes a deck of cards from the drawer of the sewing table and shuffles the cards.*) Think of it, the doctor is allowed to have the garrison band—for his private party!

THE CAPTAIN: (*Angrily.*) That's because he fawns on the Colonel in the city. Fawns, do you hear!—If I could only do that. . . .

ALICE: (*Dealing the cards.*) The doctor's wife, Gerda, and I were friends once; but she turned out to be deceitful. . . .

THE CAPTAIN: They are all false—all of them!—What's trumps? What's that card over there?

ALICE: Put on your spectacles!

THE CAPTAIN: It's no use. . . . Well, well. . . .

ALICE: Spades are trumps.

THE CAPTAIN: (*Displeased.*) Spades?

ALICE: (*Starting the game, she plays a card.*) Be that as it may—but, in any case, as far as the wives of the newly arrived officers are concerned, we are marked for ostracism.

THE CAPTAIN: (*Plays a card and takes a trick.*) What does it matter? We never give parties anyhow, so nobody will notice anything. I can stand being left alone. I have always kept to myself in the past.

ALICE: So have I. But the children. . . . The children will grow up without any companionship.

THE CAPTAIN: Let them find companions for themselves—in the city.—That's my trick. Have you another trump?

ALICE: I have one left. This trick is mine.

THE CAPTAIN: Six and eight makes fifteen. . . .

ALICE: Fourteen—fourteen!

THE CAPTAIN: Six and eight gives me fourteen. . . . I think I have forgotten how to count, too.—And two makes sixteen. . . . (*He yawns.*) It's your turn to deal.

11

ALICE: You are tired.

THE CAPTAIN: *(Dealing.)* Not at all.

ALICE: *(Listening, her ear cocked toward the open door.)* You can hear the music all the way here. *(There is a pause.)* Do you think Kurt is invited?

THE CAPTAIN: He arrived this morning, so he should have had time to get settled and unpack his evening clothes—even if he hasn't found time to call on *us*.

ALICE: Quarantine master. . . . is there to be a quarantine station here?

THE CAPTAIN: Yes.

ALICE: He is, after all, my cousin—we had the same family name. . . .

THE CAPTAIN: That's nothing to brag about!

ALICE: *(Sharply.)* Now—you leave my family alone, if you wish me to leave yours alone!

THE CAPTAIN: Now, now—are we going to start that all over again?

ALICE: Does a quarantine master have to be a physician?

THE CAPTAIN: No, he is merely a sort of civilian administrator or record-keeper; and Kurt never really made the grade.

ALICE: Kurt was always a weakling. . . .

THE CAPTAIN: . . . And has cost me a good deal of money. And when he abandoned his wife and children, it was a disgrace.

ALICE: You should not be so severe, Edgar.

THE CAPTAIN: Yes, it was scandalous. And what has he been doing in America since then? Well, I can't say I am looking forward to seeing him with any great joy; although as a young man he was agreeable enough—and I used to like to argue with him. . . .

ALICE: Because he would always yield to you!

THE CAPTAIN: *(Haughtily.)* Whether he gave in or not, he was nevertheless someone you could converse with. Here on this island I can't find a single person who comprehends what I am talking about. . . . It's a collection of idiots.

ALICE: Isn't it strange, though, that Kurt should arrive here

12

just at the time of our silver wedding—whether we now celebrate it, or not?

THE CAPTAIN: Why is that so strange?—Oh, I see—yes, of course, it was he who brought us together, or married you off, as it was said.

ALICE: Well, he did, didn't he?

THE CAPTAIN: Yes, of course, he did. It was one of those ideas of his. . . .

ALICE: A giddy idea!

THE CAPTAIN: For which *we* have had to suffer—not *he!*

ALICE: Yes. Just think, if I had remained in the theatre! All of my women friends are now stars.

THE CAPTAIN: (*Rising.*) Well, well, well. . . . Now I'll have my drink of whiskey! (*He goes to the cabinet and mixes himself a drink, which he sips standing.*) We ought to have a rail here so that one could imagine oneself in Copenhagen—at the American Bar.

ALICE: We'll have one made; if for no other reason, to remind us of Copenhagen. For, after all, there is where we had our best moments.

THE CAPTAIN: (*Gulping down his drink violently.*) Yes—do you remember Nimb's *navarin aux pommes,* do you? Superb!
(*He smacks his lips.*)

ALICE: No, but I remember the concerts at the Tivoli.

THE CAPTAIN: You are so fastidious in your tastes.

ALICE: That ought to please you, having a wife with good taste.

THE CAPTAIN: It does.

ALICE: Whenever you feel it necessary to boast about her!

THE CAPTAIN: (*Drinks.*) They must be dancing over at the doctor's—I can hear the three-quarter time of the brass tubas —boom—boom-boom. . . .

ALICE: I can hear the strains of the *Alcazar Waltz*—from beginning to end. . . . Alas, it wasn't yesterday I last danced. . . .

THE CAPTAIN: You think you are still able to dance a waltz, do you?

ALICE: Still, you say?

THE CAPTAIN: Yes. . . . Your dancing days are over—yours as well as mine.

ALICE: I am ten years younger than you, remember!

THE CAPTAIN: Then we are both the same age, for the feminine half should always be ten years younger.

ALICE: Stop your impudence! You are an old man, and I am still in my best years.

THE CAPTAIN: Yes, yes, I know that if you want to, you can be very charming—to others. . . .

ALICE: Should we light the lamps now?

THE CAPTAIN: You may as well.

ALICE: Will you ring, then. . . .

(The Captain walks sluggishly to the writing table and rings.—Jenny enters a moment later from the left.)

THE CAPTAIN: Jenny, will you be good enough to light the lamp.

ALICE: *(In a sharp tone of voice.)* I want you to light the hanging lamp.

JENNY: Yes, madam.

(She lights the hanging lamp. The Captain watches her.)

ALICE: *(Curtly; harshly.)* Have you wiped the chimney properly?

JENNY: It's clean enough.

ALICE: What kind of answer is that?

THE CAPTAIN: Now, now Alice. . . .

ALICE: *(To Jenny.)* You may leave. I'll light the lamp myself. It's much better that I do it.

JENNY: I think so, too.

(She goes toward the door.)

ALICE: *(Gets up.)* Leave!

JENNY: *(Lingering.)* I wonder what you'd say, madam, if I did leave?

(Alice is silent. Jenny goes out. The Captain steps over and lights the lamp.)

ALICE: *(Worried.)* Do you think she means to leave?

THE CANTAIN: It wouldn't surprise me. And then we'd be in a predicament.

ALICE: It's you who are to blame. You spoil them.

14

THE CAPTAIN: I do nothing of the sort. Don't you see how respectful they always are to me?

ALICE: Yes, because you fuss over them. Besides, you toady to all your subordinates; and that's because you are by nature a slave, and therefore a despot.

THE CAPTAIN: You don't say!

ALICE: Yes—you cringe before your men and your non-commissioned officers, but you can't get on with your equals and your superiors.

THE CAPTAIN: Ugh!

ALICE: You are like all tyrants. . . . Do you think she will leave?

THE CAPTAIN: She will—if you don't go out and say a friendly word to her.

ALICE: I?

THE CAPTAIN: If I went out, you'd say I was flirting with the maids.

ALICE: But think—if she should. . . . Then I would have to do all the work in the house, just like the last time, and my hands would be spoiled.

THE CAPTAIN: That wouldn't be the worst! But if Jenny goes, Kristin goes, too; and after that we would never be able to get another servant to come out to this island again. The mate on the steamboat scares away any newcomer on her way to seek employment with us. And if he does not do it, then my gunners will attend to it.

ALICE: Yes, your gunners—whom I have to feed in my kitchen just because you haven't the guts to show them the door.

THE CAPTAIN: No—for then they, too, would leave us in the lurch when their enlistment period was up; and then we would have to close up shop.

ALICE: That would be our ruin!

THE CAPTAIN: And that's why the Officers Corps is planning to petition the Crown for a special subsistence appropriation.

ALICE: Subsistence for whom?

THE CAPTAIN: For the gunners.

ALICE: (Laughs.) You are nothing short of crackbrained!

THE CAPTAIN: That's right, laugh a little for me! It does me good to hear!

ALICE: I have almost forgotten how to laugh. . . .

THE CAPTAIN: *(Lighting his cigar.)* You must never forget how to laugh. . . . Life is boring enough without it.

ALICE: It certainly is not much fun. . . . Do you want to continue the game?

THE CAPTAIN: No, I've had enough.

ALICE: You know, it frankly irritates me that the new quarantine master—who, after all, is my cousin—should visit enemies of ours the very first day he is here.

THE CAPTAIN: Well, forget about it!

ALICE: Yes, but did you see the notice in the newspaper about his arrival? They spoke of him as a man of means. He must have come into money.

THE CAPTAIN: A man of means? So-o? A rich relation! Certainly he is the first and only one in *this* family. . . .

ALICE: In your family, yes. We have had many rich men in *my* family.

THE CAPTAIN: If he has come into money, I suppose he is overbearing; but I'll hold him in check—and I won't give him a peek at my cards.

(The telegraph apparatus starts clicking.)

ALICE: Who can that be?

THE CAPTAIN: *(Remains still.)* Quiet, please.

ALICE: Go over there and listen!

THE CAPTAIN: I can hear—It's the children . . .

(He goes over to the apparatus and taps out an answer; the clicking continues for a while, after which the Captain again answers.)

ALICE: Well?

THE CAPTAIN: Wait a little . . . *(He taps out the concluding signal.)* It was the children—they are at headquarters in the city. Judith is ailing again and is staying home from school.

ALICE: Again?—What else did they say?

THE CAPTAIN: Money, as usual.

ALICE: Why must Judith be in such a hurry to graduate? It would be time enough if she took her examinations next year.

THE CAPTAIN: Tell her that, and you'll see how much good it does.

ALICE: *You* ought to tell her.

THE CAPTAIN: How many times haven't I done so! But you should know by this time that children do as they please.

ALICE: At any rate, in this house. *(The Captain yawns.)* Must you yawn?

THE CAPTAIN: What else is there for me to do? Hasn't it occurred to you that we keep repeating the very same things to each other, day after day? When you a moment ago delivered your old stand-by-reply: "At any rate, in *this* house," I should have answered with *my* old stand-by: "It is not my house alone." But as I have already delivered this speech well over a hundred times, I yawn instead. My yawning may then signify that I am either too bored to answer, or it may mean: "You are right, my angel," or: "Let's put an end to this."

ALICE: You are really quite amiable tonight.

THE CAPTAIN: Isn't it time for dinner soon?

ALICE: Did you know that the doctor and his wife have ordered supper tonight from Grand Hôtel in the city?

THE CAPTAIN: You don't say! Then they'll be having woodcock! Superb! Woodcock, you know, of all birds is the greatest delicacy. . . . but to roast it in pigs' fat is nothing short of barbaric, uncivilized.

ALICE: Ugh! Stop talking about food!

THE CAPTAIN: How about wine, then? I wonder what those barbarians are having with their woodcock?

ALICE: Would you like me to play for you?

THE CAPTAIN: *(Seating himself at the writing table.)* The last straw! Yes—if you will stop playing those funeral dirges and lamentations of yours. . . . It always sounds as if you picked your selections with a view to the effect they have on me.

And as an obligato I have to hear your eternal cry: "Oh, I am so unhappy! Miaow, miaow! What a terrible husband I have! Grumble, grumble! Oh, if he would only die! . . . Rapturous rolling of drums, and fanfares!—and at the end the *Alcazar Waltz* and the *Champagne Galop!*" Speaking of champagne, I think we have two bottles left, haven't we? Shall we have them brought up and make believe we have company? Shall we?

ALICE: No, we shall not—for it's my champagne—it was a present to me.

THE CAPTAIN: You are always so frugal.

ALICE: And you are always so miserly—to your wife, at least!

THE CAPTAIN: Then I don't know what else to propose.—Perhaps you would like me to dance for you?

ALICE: No, thanks! Your dancing days are over . . .

THE CAPTAIN: You ought to ask some woman friend to come and stay with you.

ALICE: Thanks!—You should invite one of your men friends here.

THE CAPTAIN: Thanks—that's been tried, and to our mutual dissatisfaction. But interesting as the experiment may have been, the upshot of it was that the moment a guest arrived, we were happy—that is, at first. . . .

ALICE: And then. . . .

THE CAPTAIN: Oh, let's not talk about it!

     (There is a knock at the door, right.)

ALICE: Who can that be—at this late hour?

THE CAPTAIN: Jenny is not in the habit of knocking.

ALICE: Go over and open, and don't shout "Come in!"—the way they do in workshops. . . .

THE CAPTAIN: *(Going toward the door on the right.)* You don't like workshops, eh?

     (Another knock is heard.)

ALICE: Open then, open!

THE CAPTAIN: *(Opens. A visiting card is handed to him.)* It's Kristin. . . . *(To Kristin, who remains unseen.)* Has Jenny left?

18

(The answer is not heard.)

(To Alice.)

Jenny has left!

ALICE: So now I am a domestic again!

THE CAPTAIN: And I the handy man.

ALICE: Could we get one of your gunners to help in the kitchen?

THE CAPTAIN: Not these days.

ALICE: But the card? It couldn't have been Jenny's card that Kristin handed to you!

(The Captain puts on his eyeglasses and glances at the card, then hands it to Alice.)

THE CAPTAIN: You read it, I can't. . . .

ALICE: *(Reading the card.)* Kurt! Why, it's Kurt! Go out and ask him to come in!

THE CAPTAIN: *(Goes outside, right.)* Kurt! Well, what a pleasure!

(Alice, seemingly come to life, is seen arranging her hair.—The Captain enters from the right with Kurt.)

Here is our renegade! Welcome, old boy! Let's give him a hug!

ALICE: *(Coming up to Kurt.)* Welcome to my home, Kurt!

KURT: Thank you. . . . It's a long time since we have seen one another.

THE CAPTAIN: How many years is it? Fifteen years! Old age is setting in. . . .

ALICE: Oh, Kurt looks the same as ever, it seems to me.

THE CAPTAIN: Sit down, sit down. . . . And, first of all, have you any plans for the evening? Are you invited anywhere?

KURT: I have an invitation from the doctor, but I haven't promised to come.

ALICE: In that case, you must stay with your relatives.

KURT: That would seem to be the natural thing to do—but the doctor is my superior, in a way, and it might cause me embarrassment if I didn't go.

THE CAPTAIN: What kind of nonsense is that? *I* have never had any fear of my superiors. . . .

KURT: Afraid or not, embarrassments will always crop up . . .

19

THE CAPTAIN: Here on the island, I am the master. Take refuge behind my back, then no one will dare touch you.

ALICE: Now be quiet, Edgar! *(She takes hold of Kurt's hand.)* Neither superiors nor others are going to keep you from staying with us. It is both fitting and correct that you should.

KURT: Very well, then.—Especially since I find myself so welcome here.

THE CAPTAIN: Why shouldn't you be welcome? There is no dissension between us, is there?

   (Kurt shows he is a little embarrassed.)

   Why should there be? You were a little careless once, when you were young—but all that has been forgotten. I never hold grudges.

   (Alice shows irritation. All three sit down at the sewing table.)

ALICE: Well, you have been travelling far and wide, haven't you, Kurt?

KURT: *(To Alice.)* Yes, and now I find refuge with you . . .

THE CAPTAIN: . . . whom you married off twenty-five years ago.

KURT: That isn't the precise truth, but it doesn't matter. I am glad to see that you have stuck together this many years.

THE CAPTAIN: Yes, we have dragged along . . . sometimes only so-so, but nonetheless we have stuck it out. And Alice has no cause to complain. We have had plenty of everything, and no lack of money. Perhaps you don't know that I am now a celebrated author—an author of textbooks. . . .

KURT: Yes, I recall that when we last saw each other you had had a manual of rifle instruction published and told me it had a good sale. Is it still being used in the military schools?

THE CAPTAIN: It is still used and holds its own against a second-rate work which they have tried to substitute for it, and which is totally worthless—but nonetheless finds a market . . .

   (There is a painful silence.)

KURT: You have done some travelling abroad, I hear.

ALICE: Oh yes—we have been to Copenhagen five times! Think of it!

THE CAPTAIN: Yes, you see, when I took Alice from the theatre . . .

ALICE: *(Bitingly.)* Oh, you *took* me, did you?

THE CAPTAIN: Yes, I took you—the way a wife should be taken. . . .

ALICE: How intrepid and gallant you have grown!

THE CAPTAIN: But as my wife soon after hurled the taunt at me that I had meddled with and ruined her brilliant stage career—h'm—I had to make restitution for it by promising to take her to Copenhagen. And this promise I have kept —kept dutifully. We have made five trips there. Five!

(Holds up his hand, the fingers spread apart.)

Have you ever been in Copenhagen?

KURT: *(With a smile.)* No, I have spent most of my time in America.

THE CAPTAIN: America? That must be a horribly uncivilized country, isn't it?

KURT: *(Unpleasantly affected.)* It is not Copenhagen.

ALICE: Have you—have you heard anything of your—your children?

KURT: No.

ALICE: Forgive me, Kurt dear, but wasn't it a little rash of you to leave them the way you did? . . .

KURT: I did not abandon them—they were awarded to the mother by the Court . . .

THE CAPTAIN: Let us not bring up that subject now. . . . For my part, I think it was a good thing that you got out of that mess.

KURT: *(To Alice.)* How are *your* children?

ALICE: They are well, thank you. They go to school in the city and will soon be grown up.

THE CAPTAIN: Yes, they are both fine youngsters, and the boy has a brilliant head. Brilliant! He is bound for the General Staff . . .

ALICE: If they'll accept him.

THE CAPTAIN: Accept him? Why, he has the makings of a Minister of War in him!

21

KURT: From one thing to another—there is to be a quarantine station here—for the plague, cholera, and so forth—and the Doctor, as you know, will be my superior. What sort of man is this doctor?

THE CAPTAIN: Man, you say? He is not a man—he is an illiterate blackguard!

KURT: *(To Alice.)* That makes it very disagreeable for me . . .

ALICE: Oh, he is not as bad as Edgar says, but I can't deny that to me he is anything but sympathetic.

THE CAPTAIN: He is a scoundrel, a scoundrel! And that goes for the rest of them, too,—the customs officer, the postmaster, the female telephone operator, the apothecary, the pilot, the . . . the—whatever they call it—the alderman—or councilman . . . they are all scoundrels—every one of them, and that's why I refuse to have anything to do with them.

KURT: Are you at loggerheads with all of them?

THE CAPTAIN: All of them! All!

ALICE: Yes, it's true—one can't associate with any of these people.

THE CAPTAIN: It is as if all the tyrants in the land had been sent to this island—it's a concentration camp!

ALICE: *(With irony.)* There you speak the truth!

THE CAPTAIN: *(Goodnaturedly.)* H'm. Are you alluding to me, eh? I am no tyrant—at any rate, not in my home . . .

ALICE: You had better not be!

THE CAPTAIN: *(To Kurt.)* Don't believe everything she says. I am a very well-behaved and reasonable husband, and the old woman here is the best wife in the world.

ALICE: Would you like something to drink, Kurt?

KURT: No, thank you, not just now.

THE CAPTAIN: *(With a touch of sarcasm.)* You haven't turned. . . . Have you?

KURT: Simply a little moderate, that's all.

THE CAPTAIN: The American habit, eh?

KURT: Yes.

THE CAPTAIN: None of that for me! If I can't drink all I want, then I leave it alone. A man should be able to hold his liquor.

KURT: But, to return to our neighbors here on the island. . . . In my position I shall come in contact with them all—and it won't be easy to stay clear of the rocks. No matter how hard you try to avoid entanglements, you can't help being drawn into other people's intrigues.

ALICE: By all means, Kurt, mix freely with them; you will always come back to us, for in us you have your true friends.

KURT: Don't you find it dismal to sit here so aloof—marooned among enemies?

ALICE: It is not pleasant.

THE CAPTAIN: It is not dismal at all. I have had nothing but enemies all my life; and instead of being a hindrance, they have been a help to me. And when my time comes to die, I can truthfully say that I am indebted to no one, and that no one has ever given me anything. Everything I have gained, I have had to fight for.

ALICE: Yes, Edgar's career has been no path of roses . . .

THE CAPTAIN: No—of thorns, and rocks—rocks of flint. . . . By my own strength and stamina—if you know what I mean?

KURT: (Simply.) Indeed. I came to recognize my own deficiencies in that respect ten years ago.

THE CAPTAIN: Then you are a weakliing.

ALICE: (To the Captain.) Edgar!

THE CAPTAIN: Yes, he is a weakling if he is lacking in guts and will-power. It's true, of course, that when the mechanism ceases to function, all that remains of us is a barrowful, to be dumped on some flowerbed in a garden. But while the mechanism functions, you have to kick and fight with hands and feet as long as there is life in you! That's my philosophy.

KURT: (With a smile.) Your discourse is entertaining.

THE CAPTAIN: But you don't believe it's really so?

KURT: No, I don't.

THE CAPTAIN: Nevertheless it is.

(It has commenced to be windy outside during the pre-

23

ceding scene, and suddenly one of the French windows slams shut. The Captain gets up.)

It's beginning to be windy. I felt it coming.

(He goes over and closes the doors, then taps the barometer.)

ALICE: *(To Kurt.)* You will stay for dinner, won't you?

KURT: Yes, thank you.

ALICE: It'll be very simple—our maid has just left us.

KURT: I am not finicky.

ALICE: You are so easy to please, Kurt dear.

THE CAPTAIN: *(By the barometer.)* If you could only see how the barometer is falling! Yes, I could feel it was coming.

ALICE: *(To Kurt, unobserved by the Captain.)* He is nervous.

THE CAPTAIN: It's about time we had dinner. . . .

ALICE: *(Getting up.)* I am just going out to see about it. You two sit and philosophize.

(In an aside to Kurt.)

Don't contradict him—then he'll be offended and lose his temper. And whatever you do, don't ask him why he hasn't been promoted to major!

(Kurt nods understandingly. Alice goes out, left.)

THE CAPTAIN: *(Seating himself at the sewing table, near Kurt.)* And see to it that we get something good to eat, old girl.

ALICE: Let me have some money, then, and you'll get your wish.

THE CAPTAIN: *(Handing her some money.)* Forever money. . . .

(Alice goes out.)

Money, money money! From morning till night I go about opening my purse. It has gotten to be such a habit that I have come to imagine myself being a purse. . . . Can you understand how a feeling like that can take hold of you?

KURT: Yes, I can—but with this difference that I fancied myself being a wallet.

THE CAPTAIN: Haha! So you, too, have had your experiences? Ah, these women! Haha! And you certainly picked the right kind, didn't you?

KURT: *(Without rancor.)* No use bringing that up now!

THE CAPTAIN: She was a regular jewel! . . . Well, no matter what

24

you may say, I got myself a *good* woman—for, despite everything, she is honest and reliable.

Kurt: *(With a goodnatured smile.)* Despite everything . . . ?

The Captain: Don't laugh!

Kurt: *(As before.)* Despite everything. . . .

The Captain: Yes, she has been a faithful wife—excellent mother—really splendid, but *(Glancing toward the door, left)* she has a diabolical temper. Do you know—there have been times when I have cursed you for harnessing me to her.

Kurt: *(Goodnaturedly.)* But I didn't!—Listen to me, Edgar. . . .

The Captain: Cha-cha-cha! All you talk is twaddle and you conveniently forget things that are unpleasant to remember. You mustn't be offended—I am accustomed to giving orders and commands and to be blustering. . . . But you know me, and you won't take offense, will you?

Kurt: Certainly not. But I did not harness you to your wife—quite the contrary.

The Captain: *(Without letting Kurt interrupt him in his tirade.)* Don't you really think life is strange?

Kurt: It is, indeed.

The Captain: And that we should have to grow old! It is no fun, but it is interesting. . . . I am not really old, yet I am beginning to feel my years. One by one your acquaintances die off, and you are left desolate, companionless.

Kurt: The man who can grow old with a woman by his side, is indeed fortunate.

The Captain: Fortunate? Yes, it is fortunate—for your children leave you, too. You should never have left your children.

Kurt: Yes, but I didn't. They were taken from me.

The Captain: You must not be angry when I say this to you.

Kurt: But such was not the case!

The Captain: Well, whichever way it was, it is all forgotten. But you *are* alone.

Kurt: We get used to anything and everything, my dear Edgar.

The Captain: Do you think one can. . . . Can one get used also to be—to be completely alone?

Kurt: Look at me!

25

THE CAPTAIN: What have you been doing these fifteen years?

KURT: What a question to ask! These fifteen years. . . .

THE CAPTAIN: I hear you have come into money and are rich.

KURT: I am not rich.

THE CAPTAIN: I have no intention of borrowing. . . .

KURT: If you had, I wouldn't refuse you.

THE CAPTAIN: That's very generous of you, but I always try to make both ends meet. You see. . . .

(With a glance toward the door on the left.)

. . . here in this house there must be no lack of anything; and the day there was no more money—she would leave me!

KURT: Oh no!

THE CAPTAIN: No? Well, I know better!—Will you believe it— whenever I am out of money, that is the time she pounces on me, simply to give her the satisfaction of showing me that I am failing to support my family.

KURT: But I remember you told me you had an ample income.

THE CAPTAIN: So I have—I have a large income; still it is not enough.

KURT: Then it is not really large—generally speaking.

THE CAPTAIN: Life is strange; and so are we. . . .

(The telegraph apparatus starts clicking.)

KURT: What is that?

THE CAPTAIN: Just a routine time signal.

KURT: Have you no telephone?

THE CAPTAIN: Yes, in the kitchen. But *we* use the telegraph because the telephone girls blab everything we say.

KURT: You must lead a dreadful life out here in this community by the sea. . . .

THE CAPTAIN: Yes, it's nothing short of horrible. And life itself is horrible. But you, who believe in a life after this, do you really think you will find peace in the hereafter?

KURT: No doubt we shall have storm and struggle there also.

THE CAPTAIN: There also—if there is a hereafter! But rather than that, annihilation!

KURT: How do you know that annihilation will come without pain?

26

THE CAPTAIN: When I die, I am going to go like that! (*He snaps his fingers.*) Without any pain!

KURT: Are you so sure of that?

THE CAPTAIN: Yes, I am.

KURT: You don't seem to be satisfied with your life?

THE CAPTAIN: (*With a sigh.*) Satisfied? The day I die I shall be satisfied!

KURT: (*Rising.*) That is something you don't know.—But tell me—just what is going on in this house?—What takes place here? There is an odor as if the wallpaper were poisoned; you feel sick the moment you come inside. . . . Had I not promised Alice to stay, I would leave this place without hesitation. There is a corpse buried here—and I feel a hate here so venomous that I can hardly breathe.

(*The Captain collapses in his chair and stares into spare.*)

What is wrong, Edgar?

(*The Captain remains motionless. Kurt pats him on the shoulder.*)

Edgar!

THE CAPTAIN: (*Recovering somewhat, he glances about.*) Eh? Did you say something? I thought I heard Alice. . . . Oh, it's you? Tell me. . . .

(*He relapses into insensibility.*)

KURT: This is frightful.

(*He goes over to the door on the left and opens it.*)

Alice!

ALICE: (*Comes in; she is wearing a kitchen apron.*) What is the matter, Kurt?

KURT: I don't know. . . . Look at him!

ALICE: (*Calmly.*) His mind goes blank like that once in a while.—I'll play something. That will wake him.

(*She walks over to the piano.*)

KURT: No, no—leave him to me. . . . Can he hear us? Can he see?

ALICE: Just now he can neither hear nor see.

KURT: And you say that so calmly!—Alice, what is going on in this house?

27

ALICE: Ask him there!

KURT: Him there, you say! Why, he is your husband!

ALICE: To me he is a stranger—as much a stranger as he was twenty-five years ago. I know nothing whatsoever about that man other than that. . . .

KURT: Sh! He may hear you. . . .

ALICE: He can't hear.

> (*The sound of a bugle is heard from without. The Captain leaps to his feet and snatches his sabre and cap.*)

THE CAPTAIN: Excuse me! I have to inspect the guard!

> (*He rushes out through the French doors.*)

KURT: Does he suffer from some illness?

ALICE: I don't know.

KURT: Is he mentally disturbed?

ALICE: I don't know.

KURT: Does he drink?

ALICE: He boasts more about his drinking than actually doing it.

KURT: Sit down and tell me all—but calmly and truthfully.

ALICE: (*Sits down.*) What can I tell you?—that I have spent a lifetime in this tower, this prison, guarded by a man I have always hated, whom I still hate so boundlessly that I would laugh wildly the moment he gave up the ghost.

KURT: Why haven't you divorced him?

ALICE: That's a good question! We broke off our engagement twice—and ever since, we have been trying to get away from each other. But we are welded together and we can't break the link. We did separate once—living apart here in this house—for five years. Now only death can part us—and we know it—and that is why we keep waiting for death as our deliverer.

KURT: Why have you no one you can associate with?

ALICE: Because he keeps me isolated. First he rooted out my brothers and sisters from our home—he used that very word: root out—and after that he did the same to my women friends and others.

KURT: But what about *his* relations? Did *you* remove them?

ALICE: Yes—for after stripping me of my good name and honor, they very nearly robbed me of my life. Finally I was forced to rely upon that telegraph apparatus over there as my only contact with people and the world outside—for the telephone girls listened in and kept us from using that convenience. He is unaware that I have taught myself to tap out messages; and you must not mention it to him. He would kill me if he knew.

KURT: Horrible—horrible!—But why does he reproach me for having married you off to him? Let me tell you how it came about. . . . Edgar and I were childhood friends. The moment he saw you, he fell in love with you. And he came to me and asked me to intercede for him. I promptly refused—I was aware of your domineering and unfeeling nature, dear Alice. And I warned him. But when he nonetheless persisted, I told him to go to your brother and ask him to speak for him.

ALICE: I believe what you say; but since he has been deceiving himself for all these years, you will never get him to believe anything else.

KURT: Well, then let him put the blame on me—if that will ease the pain for him.

ALICE: But that is more than. . . .

KURT: I am used to it. . . . But what *does* wound my feelings is his unjust imputation that I have deserted my children.

ALICE: That is the way he is—he says whatever he feels like saying; and having said it, he believes it. Yet he seems to have an attachment for you, because you don't contradict him. . . . But please try not to get tired of us now! That you should have come at this very time was indeed fortunate for us, a stroke of fate, I believe. . . . Kurt, you must not get tired of us, for in all the world I don't think there are two beings more miserable than we.

(She weeps.)

KURT: I have seen one marriage at close quarters—and that was appalling! But this is almost worse!

ALICE: Is that what you think?

KURT: Yes.

ALICE: Who is to blame?

KURT: Alice! If you will stop asking who is to blame, it will help to ease your mind. Try to look upon it as a fact, a trial, which must be borne.

ALICE: I can't do it! It is too much to bear! *(She gets up.)* There is no help for it!

KURT: I pity you both!—Do you know why you hate each other?

ALICE: No—it is the most senseless hate—there is no ground for it—completely uncalled for—and there will be no end to it. And do you know why he so vehemently hates to die? He is afraid I'll get married again!

KURT: Then he still loves you.

ALICE: I suppose so. But that doesn't deter him from hating me.

KURT: *(As if speaking to himself.)* They call it love-hate, and it stems from the bottom of hell.—Does he derive any pleasure from your playing for him?

ALICE: Yes, but he only likes horrid pieces—such as for instance that ghastly 'The Entry of the Boyars'. Whenever I play that, he starts behaving as though he were possessed and wants to dance.

KURT: He dances?

ALICE: Yes, he acts quite silly at times.

KURT: If you'll forgive me, there is one thing I would like to ask you—where are your children?

ALICE: You don't know, perhaps, that two of them are dead?

KURT: So you have had to suffer that, too?

ALICE: Is there anything I haven't been through?

KURT: But where are the other two children?

ALICE: In the city; I could not have them at home—he incited them against me.

KURT: And you did the same, didn't you?

ALICE: Why, certainly. And so there was partisanship and prejudice—bribes and vote buying; and in order not to corrupt the children we had to send them away. What was to have been a bond uniting us, became instead a sword between us; what was to have been the blessings of a home turned out to be a curse. . . . Yes, there are times when I think there is a curse upon our whole family!

KURT: Yes, ever since the Fall—yes.

ALICE: *(With a venomous glance and sharpness of voice.)* Which fall?

KURT: The parents of mankind.

ALICE: Oh—I thought you referred to some other fall! *(There is a moment of silent embarrassment. Alice wrings her hands.)* Kurt! You are my cousin, my childhood friend. . . . I have not always behaved toward you as I should have; but now that you see me receiving my punishment, you have been given your revenge.

KURT: No, no, not revenge! It's not in my nature—no, no!

ALICE: Do you recall one Sunday when you were engaged and I had invited you to dine with us?

KURT: Sh! Sh!

ALICE: No, no, I must speak! Do be lenient with me! . . . When you arrived we were not at home, and you had to turn about and go home.

KURT: You had been invited out yourselves. . . . But why bring all this up now?

ALICE: Kurt! When I just now invited you to stay for dinner, I thought there was enough food in the house. . . . *(She covers her face with her hands.)* . . . but there isn't a thing— not as much as a crust of bread!

KURT: My poor, poor Alice!

ALICE: And now—when he comes home and wants his dinner and finds there isn't any, he'll fly into a rage. You have never seen him in a rage! Oh God, what a humiliating existence!

KURT: Why don't you let me go and straighten out this whole thing?

ALICE: There is nothing to be bought on this island.

KURT: Not for my sake, but for his—and your own sake—let me think up something—something. . . . We must treat the whole matter with levity—we must laugh over it when he

31

comes back. . . . I'll propose that we all have a drink—and in the meantime, I'll get some sort of idea. . . . We'll put him in a good humor—play for him—any kind of trash. . . . You sit down at the piano now and be prepared.

ALICE: Look at my hands! How can I play with such hands? I have to polish the brass, do the dishes, tidy up the house, make the fires, and. . . .

KURT: But you have two servants, haven't you?

ALICE: We have to say we have two because he is an officer—but they are always leaving so that we are sometimes—most of the time—without any. . . . I don't know how to get out of this—this predicament with the dinner? Oh, I wish the house would go up in smoke!

KURT: Alice! Alice! Don't!

ALICE: Or that the sea would roll in and swallow us!

KURT: No, Alice! No, I won't listen to you!

ALICE: What will he say? What will he say? Don't leave me, Kurt, don't leave me!

KURT: My poor Alice! No—I shan't leave you!

ALICE: Yes—but after you have gone. . . .

KURT: Has he ever struck you?

ALICE: Struck me? Oh no! Then I would leave him—and he knows it! I hope I have *some* pride left!

> *(From outside can be heard the challenge of the sentry: "Halt! Who goes there?" and the answer: "Friend.")*

KURT: *(Rising.)* Is that he coming?

ALICE: *(Frightened.)* Yes, that's he!

> *(There is a silence.)*

KURT: What in the world shall we do?

ALICE: I don't know—I don't know!

THE CAPTAIN: *(Enters from the rear; he is in a jovial mood.)* Now that's done! Free again! Well, has she had time to weather her troubles, eh? Doesn't she lead a dreadful life, eh?

KURT: How is the weather outside, Edgar?

THE CAPTAIN: Stiff gale! *(Jestingly he opens one of the doors slightly.*) Sir Bluebeard and the maiden in the tower—and outside the sentry paces back and forth with drawn sword, keeping watch over the fair one. And then the brothers arrive. But the sentry is at his post, doing his duty! Look at him! Hip, hip! One, two; one, two! He is on the alert! Look at him! Melitam-tam-ta—melita-lee-ah-li! Let's have the sword dance—I want Kurt to see it!

KURT: No, let's have 'The Entry of the Boyars' instead.

THE CAPTAIN: You know that, do you?—Alice-in-the-kitchen-apron, come and play! Come on, I say! (*Alice goes reluctantly to the piano. The Captain pinches her arm.*) You have been talking about me behind my back, haven't you?

ALICE: I? (*Kurt turns away from him. Alice plays 'The Entry of the Boyars.' The Captain goes into some kind of Hungarian dance, in back of the writing table, to the obligato of jingling spurs. He suddenly collapses and falls in a heap, without being noticed by Kurt and Alice. Alice continues playing and finishes the dance music, after which she—without turning—asks:*) Shall I play again? (*Silence. Alice turns around and sees the Captain lying unconscious behind the writing table, where he cannot be seen by the audience.*) God in heaven! (*She stands motionless, with arms crossed, and gives a sigh as of relief and gratitude. Kurt turns and sees what has happened, then hurries over to the Captain.*)

KURT: What's the matter? What's the matter?

ALICE: (*In an extreme state of tension.*) Is he dead?

KURT: I don't know. Help me!

ALICE: (*Standing still as before.*) I can't touch him. . . . Is he dead?

KURT: No, he is breathing.

> (*Alice gives a sigh. The Captain gets up, aided by Kurt, who places him in a chair.*)

THE CAPTAIN: What's wrong? What is it? (*Silence.*) What is it?

KURT: You fell.

THE CAPTAIN: Well, what of it?

KURT: You fell to the floor! How do you feel now?

THE CAPTAIN: How do I feel? There's nothing wrong with me! Why should there be? Why do you stand staring at me?

KURT: You are not well.

THE CAPTAIN: Stop talking nonsense! Keep on playing, Alice. . . . Oh, now it's coming back again. . . .

(His hands go to his head.)

ALICE: You see—you are ill!

THE CAPTAIN: Stop screaming—it's nothing but a touch of dizziness. . . .

KURT: We must get the Doctor for you. I'll go out to the kitchen and telephone.

THE CAPTAIN: I will have no doctor!

KURT: You must, Edgar! For our own sake, we must call him, or we'll be held responsible.

THE CAPTAIN: I'll kick him out if he comes—I'll shoot him! Oh, it's coming back. . . .

(Again his hands go to his head.)

KURT: *(Goes to the door on the left.)* I'm telephoning this minute. . . .

(He goes out. Alice removes her apron.)

THE CAPTAIN: Will you get me a glass of water?

ALICE: I suppose I have to.

(She pours him a glass of water.)

THE CAPTAIN: *(With irony.)* How tenderhearted you are!

ALICE: Are you sick?

THE CAPTAIN: Forgive me for being indisposed!

ALICE: Will you take care of yourself now?

THE CAPTAIN: I don't suppose you care to look after me.

ALICE: I certainly don't!

THE CAPTAIN: The moment you have been waiting for so long has come. . . .

ALICE: Yes—the moment you thought would never come.

THE CAPTAIN: You mustn't be angry with me.

(Kurt enters from the left.)

KURT: This is an outrage! . . .

ALICE: What did he say?

34

KURT: He hung up without even answering me!

ALICE: *(To the Captain.)* There you see the consequences of your monstrous arrogance.

THE CAPTAIN: I think I am getting sicker. . . . Try to get the doctor from the city. . . .

ALICE: *(Goes over to the telegraph apparatus.)* We'll have to use the telegraph, then.

THE CAPTAIN: *(Halfway getting up out of the chair, in consternation.)* Do—you—do you know—how to use the telegraph?

ALICE: *(Tapping the keys.)* Yes, I do.

THE CAPTAIN: So-o?—Well, go on then. . . . What a false woman! *(To Kurt.)* Come here and sit by me. . . . *(Kurt goes to him.)* Take my hand. Here I am—sitting up—yet I have the sensation of falling—falling. . . . Can you imagine—falling—as from a precipice. . . . Such a strange feeling!

KURT: Have you had similar attacks before?

THE CAPTAIN: Never.

KURT: While we are waiting for an answer from the city, I am going over to see the doctor and have a talk with him.—Has he looked after you before?

THE CAPTAIN: Yes, he has.

KURT: Then he knows your condition?

(He goes toward the right.)

ALICE: *(To Kurt.)* They'll come back with an answer shortly.—You are being awfully nice, Kurt. . . . But don't be away long. . . .

KURT: I'll be back as soon as I can.

THE CAPTAIN: Kurt is nice, isn't he? And hasn't he changed?

ALICE: Yes, and for the better. But I feel sorry that he should be dragged into our misery, just as he has come back.

THE CAPTAIN: But a lucky thing for us!—I wonder how things really are with him. Did you notice how reluctant he was to talk about his own affairs?

ALICE: I noticed it, yes; but I don't think anyone asked him about that, anyhow.

THE CAPTAIN: Just think, what a life he has led! And think of ours! I wonder if everybody leads such an existence as we do?

ALICE: Perhaps. But they don't talk about it so much.

THE CAPTAIN: There are times when I think that misery attracts misery and that people who are happy keep away from anything of an unhappy nature. That is why *we* never meet anything but misery.

ALICE: Have you ever known anyone who was really happy?

THE CAPTAIN: I'm trying to think. . . . No. . . . Yes—the Ekmarks.

ALICE: You don't mean it? But the wife was operated on last year!

THE CAPTAIN: Oh, yes, I forgot.—Well, then I can't think of anyone. . . . Yes, the von Kraffts!

ALICE: Yes, there is a family which for fifty years lived a truly bucolic life. They were all respected and well off financially, their children were well-behaved and they married well. And then that cousin of theirs committed a crime and was sent to prison. And that had consequences for the rest of them; for after that, their peaceful existence was at an end. The family name was disgraced in all the newspapers. The Krafft murder case put an end to all their social relationships; this despite the fact that they were once held in the highest esteem. And the children were forced to leave school. . . . Oh God!

THE CAPTAIN: I wonder what my sickness can be?

ALICE: Haven't you any idea?

THE CAPTAIN: It could be the heart, or the head. I feel as if my soul was trying to fly out of my body and go up into a cloud of smoke.

ALICE: How's your appetite?

THE CAPTAIN: Yes—what about dinner?

ALICE: (*Suddenly begins to pace the floor uneasily.*) I'll ask Jenny.

THE CAPTAIN: But she has left.

ALICE: Yes, yes, of course.

36

THE CAPTAIN: Ring for Kristin—I'd like to have some fresh water.

ALICE: *(Rings.)* Could *she* have . . . ?
(She rings again.)

THE CAPTAIN: Go and see. . . . She couldn't have gone, too, could she?

ALICE: *(Goes to the door on the right and opens it.)* What's this? Her trunk is in the hall—all packed.

THE CAPTAIN: Then she has gone.

ALICE: This is truly hell!
(She bursts into tears, falls to her knees and, with head resting on a chair, sobs.)

THE CAPTAIN: Everything comes at once! And just our luck that Kurt should come and find us in this muddle! If any more humiliations are in store for us, we may as well have them all come at the same time. . . .

ALICE: Do you know—something just strikes me! When Kurt went, he had no intention of coming back. . . .

THE CAPTAIN: That would not surprise me in the least!

ALICE: Yes, we are under a curse!

THE CAPTAIN: Stop talking nonsense!

ALICE: Don't you see how everybody shuns and turns away from us?

THE CAPTAIN: What do I care? *(The telegraph apparatus starts clicking.)* There is your answer now. Quiet, I want to hear. . . . No one can spare the time. . . . Evasions, excuses!—Such rabble!

ALICE: This is what you get for treating your doctors so contemptuously and always ignoring their bills

THE CAPTAIN: That is not true!

ALICE: Even when you could well afford it, you refused to pay them, because you questioned their competence—just as you looked down upon what I and others did for you.—And now they refuse to come to you. And the telephone has been cut off because you considered it unnecessary. Nothing is worth anything to you except your guns and your rifles!

37

THE CAPTAIN: Don't stand there talking rubbish!

ALICE: Everything comes back to us. . . .

THE CAPTAIN: What sort of superstition is that? You sound like an old crone.

ALICE: You will see!—We owe Kristin six months' wages—you know that.

THE CAPTAIN: She has stolen that much.

ALICE: And I have had to borrow from her, besides.

THE CAPTAIN: It doesn't surprise me at all!

ALICE: What an ungrateful person you are! You know that I borrowed the money for the children so they could get to the city.

THE CAPTAIN: *(Sarcastically.)* Kurt certainly came back, didn't he? He is another rogue. And he is weak, besides. Didn't have the courage to admit that he had had enough of us, and that he would have more fun at the Doctor's dance. I suppose he was afraid he would get a poor meal here with us. The scoundrel has really not changed very much.

KURT: *(Enters speedily from the right.)* Now, my dear Edgar, this is how the matter stands. . . . The Doctor knows every nook and cranny of your heart. . . .

THE CAPTAIN: My heart?

KURT: Yes, you have long been suffering from calcification of the heart.

THE CAPTAIN: A stony heart?

KURT: And. . . .

THE CAPTAIN: Is that something serious?

KURT: Well—it is. . . .

THE CAPTAIN: It is serious.

KURT: Yes.

THE CAPTAIN: Fatal?

KURT: You must be careful—very careful! The first thing you have to do is to stop smoking. *(The Captain throws away his cigar.)* And the next thing: no more whiskey. And then, to bed.

THE CAPTAIN: *(Alarmed.)* No—that I won't do—I refuse to go to bed. That would be the end of me! Once put to bed, you

38

never get up. . . . I am going to sleep on the sofa tonight.— What else did he say?

KURT: He acted very friendly, and if you should need him, he will answer your call without delay.

THE CAPTAIN: He was friendly, was he, the hypocrite? I have no wish to see him.—He will let me eat, at least?

KURT: Not tonight. And for the next few days, nothing but milk.

THE CAPTAIN: *(Makes a wry face.)* Milk! I can't stand the taste of it!

KURT: You had better get used to it.

THE CAPTAIN: No, I am too old to learn new tricks! *(His hands go to his head.)* Oh, there it is again. . . .

(He remains sitting in his chair staring into space.)

ALICE: *(To Kurt.)* What did the Doctor say?

KURT: That he may die—without warning.

ALICE: Thank God!

KURT: Watch yourself, Alice, watch yourself!—And now—go and get a blanket and pillow. I'm going to put him to bed here on the sofa. And I'll spend the night in that chair.

ALICE: What shall I do?

KURT: You go to bed. It seems to make him worse when you are about.

ALICE: You tell me what to do, and I'll obey, for I know you mean what is best for us both.

(She goes out, right.)

KURT: *(Calling after her as she is leaving.)* Remember—what is best for you both! I am taking no one's side in this. *(Kurt takes the water decanter and goes out, left. Outside the wind is blowing, and suddenly the French doors are blown wide open and an old woman, shabbily dressed and with ugly, horrid features, peeps into the room. The Captain is awakened, sits up, and looks about.)*

THE CAPTAIN: So-o? They walked out on me, the miserable creatures! *(He catches sight of the old woman and is terrified.)* Who are you? What do you want?

THE OLD WOMAN: I only wanted to close the door, dear sir.

THE CAPTAIN: Why close it? Why close it?

THE OLD WOMAN: Because it blew open just as I was passing.

THE CAPTAIN: You were going to steal, weren't you?

THE OLD WOMAN: Not much to steal here, Kristin tells me.

THE CAPTAIN: Kristin!

THE OLD WOMAN: Good night, sir. Sleep well. . . .

> *(She goes out, closing the doors after her.—Alice enters from the right, carrying a blanket and pillows.)*

THE CAPTAIN: Who was that at the door just now? Was anybody here?

ALICE: It was old Maja from the poorhouse—she was just passing by.

THE CAPTAIN: Are you sure that it was she?

ALICE: Are you afraid?

THE CAPTAIN: I—afraid? Of course not!

ALICE: Since you won't go to bed, lie down here, then.

THE CAPTAIN: *(Goes to the sofa and lies down.)* This is where I want to lie. *(He takes her hand, but she withdraws it. Kurt enters with the water decanter.)* Kurt! Don't leave me!

KURT: I am staying with you all night. Alice is going to bed.

THE CAPTAIN: Good night, then, Alice!

ALICE: *(To Kurt.)* Good night, Kurt!

> *(Kurt takes a chair and seats himself close by the Captain.)*

KURT: Don't you want to take off your boots, Edgar?

THE CAPTAIN: No! A soldier should always be fully armed and equipped.

KURT: Are you getting ready for a battle, then?

THE CAPTAIN: Perhaps. . . . *(He sits up.)* Kurt! You are the only one I have ever taken into my confidence. I want you to listen to me now.—If I should die tonight—look after my children!

KURT: I promise you that.

THE CAPTAIN: Thank you! I know I can trust you.

KURT: Will you tell me just why you trust me?

THE CAPTAIN: We have not been friends—I put no faith in friendship—and our two families were born enemies and have always been at war. . . .

40

KURT: And nevertheless you trust me?

THE CAPTAIN: Yes—and I don't know why I do. *(There is a silence.)* Do you think I am going to die?

KURT: You—as all of us. You are not immune.

THE CAPTAIN: Do you feel embittered?

KURT: Yes.—Are you afraid of dying? Of the wheelbarrow and the garden plot?

THE CAPTAIN: But think—if that were not the end?

KURT: Many think not.

THE CAPTAIN: And what then?

KURT: Perhaps wonder without end. . . .

THE CAPTAIN: But we have no conclusive knowledge of that.

KURT: No. that's just it! And so we have to be prepared for anything.

THE CAPTAIN: You are not childish enough to believe in a hell?

KURT: Don't you—who are living in one?

THE CAPTAIN: That's only in a figurative sense.

KURT: Your description of your own hell was realistic enough to exclude any thought of being metaphorical, whether poetic or otherwise.

(Silence.)

THE CAPTAIN: If you only knew what agony I am going through?

KURT: Physical pain?

THE CAPTAIN: No—not physical.

KURT: Then I suppose your misery is mental or spiritual—there could be no other.

(Silence.)

THE CAPTAIN: *(Sits up suddenly.)* I don't want to die!

KURT: A moment ago you were asking to be blotted out of existence.

THE CAPTAIN: Yes—if there were no pain. . . .

KURT: But it doesn't seem to be painless, does it?

THE CAPTAIN: Is this the end then?

KURT: The beginning of the end. . . .

THE CAPTAIN: Good night!

KURT: Good night!

END OF SCENE 1

41

ACT I   SCENE 2

The setting is the same as in Scene 1.

The lamp is flickering out. Through the windows and the glass panes in the French windows, Center, can be seen the overcast sky, and the sea in motion. A sentry is doing guard duty at the battery emplacement, as in the preceding scene.

The Captain is lying on the sofa, asleep. Kurt is sitting in his chair near the sofa. He looks pale and weary from lack of sleep.

ALICE: *(Enters from the right.)* Is he sleeping?

KURT: Yes, from the time the sun was due to rise.

ALICE: What kind of night did he have?

KURT: He slept by fits and starts but kept talking continually.

ALICE: About what?

KURT: He kept arguing about religion like a schoolboy; and at the same time claimed to have solved the riddle of the universe. Finally, toward morning, he had discovered the immortality of the soul.

ALICE: For his own glory!

KURT: Precisely. He is actually the most overbearing and self-opinionated person I have ever met. "I exist, therefore God must exist."

ALICE: Now you see, don't you. . . . Look at his boots! With them he would have trampled the earth flat, if he had had his way; with them he has trampled other people's fields and flowerbeds; with them he has trampled on people's toes, and on my nerves, my spirit. . . . Voracious bear! At last you have been given your deathblow!

KURT: He would have been comic had he not been so tragic; yet even in his pettiness, there is a touch of grandeur. Isn't there a single kind word you can say about him, Alice?

ALICE: *(Sits down.)* Yes—if only he doesn't hear it; for if one has one word of praise for him, he at once becomes madly overweening. *(With a nervous glance at the Captain.)*

KURT: *(Reassuring.)* He can't hear a word we say; he has been given morphine.

ALICE: Edgar was reared in a poor home. He had many brothers and sisters. In his youth he had to support the family by tutoring because his father was a good-for-nothing, or even worse. It must be hard for a young man to have to give up all the pleasures of youth and have to slave for a lot of ungrateful children whom he has not brought into the world. I was a little girl when I first saw him—he was already a young man then—going about without overcoat in the cold of winter, with the thermometer at 25° Centigrade—while his small sisters were wearing duffel coats. That was generous of him, and I admired him for it, even though I was repelled by his ugly face. Don't you think he is exceptionally ugly?

KURT: Yes, there is something repulsive about his ugliness, as you say. I noticed it particularly every time there was a break in our friendship; and when we were separated from each other, his image grew, took on hideous and formidable proportions, and he actually haunted me.

ALICE: Then think of me!—But his first three years as an officer were unquestionably a painful, difficult trial for him, although he from time to time received help from some rich benefactors. However, he would never acknowledge this, and he accepted everything he could get hold of as if it were due him—and without ever offering a word of thanks in return.

KURT: We were to speak well of him, weren't we?

ALICE: After he is dead, yes. Well, I can't remember anything more now. . . .

KURT: Have you found him ill-natured, spiteful?

ALICE: Yes—and still he can be both kind and overemotionally tender.—As an enemy he is absolutely horrible.

KURT: Why has he never been promoted to major?

ALICE: You ought to understand that yourself. Nobody wants to have a man like him as a superior, a man who—already as a subaltern—was a tyrant. But never breathe a word about that to him. He himself says he has no desire to be a major. —Did he say anything about the children to you?

KURT: Yes, he wished he could see Judith.

ALICE: I can well understand that. Do you know what Judith is like? She is his image—and he has trained her to agitate and hound and pester me. Imagine it—my own daughter— my own daughter has raised her hand against me.

KURT: Oh no! That's a little too much!

ALICE: Sh! I see him moving. . . . Just think, if he has heard what we said. . . . He is crafty, you know. . . .

KURT: *(In a subdued voice.)* He does seem to be awake.

ALICE: Doesn't he look like a troll? He frightens me!
    (There is a silence.)

THE CAPTAIN: *(Stirring, he wakes and sits up, then looks around.)* It's morning—at last!

KURT: How do you feel now?

THE CAPTAIN: Badly.

KURT: Would you like to have the Doctor?

THE CAPTAIN: No—I want to see Judith—my child!

KURT: Wouldn't it be advisable to adjust your family affairs before you . . . in case something should happen?

THE CAPTAIN: What do you mean? What could happen?

KURT: That which happens to all of us. . . .

THE CAPTAIN: What nonsense! I shan't die as quickly as you think, so don't gloat prematurely, Alice.

KURT: Think of your children, Edgar! Make your will so that your wife will at least have the furniture.

THE CAPTAIN: Is she to inherit it while I am alive?

KURT: No—but if anything were to happen, she should not have to be thrown out of house and home. Anyone who for twenty-five years has dusted and polished the furniture and kept the house in order, should be entitled to keep it.—Will you let me call the judge advocate?

44

THE CAPTAIN: No!

KURT: You are a cruel husband, more cruel than I thought!

THE CAPTAIN: *(Collapses without warning and falls backward on the sofa.)* It's coming back again. . . .
(He loses consciousness.)

ALICE: *(Walking toward the door, left.)* I hear someone in the kitchen—I have to go out there.

KURT: By all means—there is not much you can do here. *(She goes out.)*

THE CAPTAIN: *(Regaining consciousness.)* Well, Kurt, what are your plans for the quarantine station here?

KURT: Oh, everything will work out satisfactorily, I am sure.

THE CAPTAIN: Yes, but don't forget that I am in command on this island, and you will have to deal with me.

KURT: Have you ever seen a quarantine station?

THE CAPTAIN: Have I? Certainly, before you were born. And let me give you a piece of advice. Don't place the disinfecting-ovens too near the shore.

KURT: I was of the opinion that proximity to the sea would be the most favorable location.

THE CAPTAIN: That shows how much you know about it. Don't you know that water is the favorite element of bacilli—the element that gives them life?

KURT: But the salt water of the sea is essential for washing away impurities.

THE CAPTAIN: Idiot!—Well, now that you are set in your quarters, you must bring your children here.

KURT: Do you think they will yield to my entreaties?

THE CAPTAIN: Of course, if you have any kind of backbone. You would make a good impression on your associates here if they saw that you fulfilled your duties in that respect, too. . . .

KURT: I have always fulfilled my duties in that respect.

THE CAPTAIN: *(His voice growing loud.)* . . . in that respect—for it is there that you have been most neglectful.

KURT: But I have told you. . . .

THE CAPTAIN: *(Interrupting and persisting in his badgering.)* For a father does not desert his children that way. . . .

KURT: Keep right on!

THE CAPTAIN: As a relative of yours—who is also your elder—I feel I have a right and duty to speak out, even if the truth is painful to hear. And you should not be offended.

KURT: Are you hungry?

THE CAPTAIN: Yes, I am.

KURT: Would you like something light?

THE CAPTAIN: No, I want something substantial.

KURT: That would put an end to you.

THE CAPTAIN: Isn't it enough that I am sick; must I starve, too?

KURT: That's how it has to be.

THE CAPTAIN: Not even a drink—and can't smoke! Then life is not worth living. . . .

KURT: Death has to have his sacrifices, or he'll be ready with his scythe.
(Alice enters with several bouquets of flowers, a few telegrams and letters. She throws the flowers on the table.)

ALICE: These are for you.

THE CAPTAIN: *(Flattered.)* For me? Let me see!

ALICE: They are only from the non-commissioned officers, from the band, and the artillerymen.

THE CAPTAIN: You are envious.

ALICE: Anything but that! Had they sent you a laurel wreath —that would have been a different matter. But they would never give you one of those.

THE CAPTAIN: H'm. Here is a telegram from the Colonel. You read it, Kurt. . . . I must admit he is a gentleman, no matter what you say . . . even if he is a bit of an idiot.—Here is one from. . . . what does it say? It's from Judith. . . . Telegraph her, please, and ask her to come out by the next boat.—And this—well, I see I am not entirely without friends, and it pleases me that they give me a thought when I am sick; after all, I think I deserve it, being a man without fear or favor, and far superior to his rank. . . .

46

ALICE: I don't quite understand—are they congratulating you because you are sick?

THE CAPTAIN: Hyena!

ALICE: *(To Kurt.)* You know, we had a medical officer here on the island who was so disliked that when he was leaving, he was given a banquet. But it was not a farewell affair in the usual sense; it was given in celebration of his departure!

THE CAPTAIN: Put the flowers in vases. . . . I don't think anyone can accuse me of being gullible—and people are all a lot of riff-raff—but, by God, these simple tributes can be nothing but heartfelt!

ALICE: Ass!

KURT: *(Reading one of the telegrams.)* Judith says she cannot come. The steamboat isn't running because of the storm.

THE CAPTAIN: Is that all?

KURT: Well, no—there is something else.

THE CAPTAIN: Out with it!

KURT: Well, she begs her father not to drink so much.

THE CAPTAIN: What impudence!—And that from my children—my own beloved daughter—my Judith, the apple of my eye!

ALICE: The image of you!

THE CAPTAIN: That is life for you! And the sweetest of its blessings! To hell with it!

ALICE: Now you are reaping the harvest of what you have sowed. You set her against her mother, and now she turns against her father. . . . Now tell me there isn't a God!

THE CAPTAIN: *(To Kurt.)* What does the Colonel have to say?

KURT: He grants you leave of absence—that's all he says.

THE CAPTAIN: Leave of absence? I have asked for no leave of absence. . . .

ALICE: But I have.

THE CAPTAIN: I refuse to accept it.

ALICE: The order has already been issued.

THE CAPTAIN: That's none of my concern!

ALICE: You see, Kurt, that for this man no laws exist—neither constitutional nor statutory, nor any prescribed authority. He is a law unto himself, above everything and everybody

—the universe was created for his personal convenience and advantage—the sun and the moon exist merely that their rays may carry his praises to the stars. That is the kind of man my husband is! The insignificant captain who could not even rise to the rank of major; at whose pomposity everybody snickers, while *he* thinks that they hold him in awe—this petty creature who is afraid of the dark and whose faith is centered in the high and low of the barometer—all this, in addition to, and as a final curtain: a barrowful of manure—and not of the best brand either.

(All through this scene the Captain has been fanning himself with a bouquet of flowers with evident self-complacency and conceit, and without paying any attention to what Alice is saying.)

THE CAPTAIN: Have you invited Kurt to have some breakfast?

ALICE: No.

THE CAPTAIN: Then fix us at once two steaks—two succulent Chateaubriands.

ALICE: Two?

THE CAPTAIN: I am having one myself.

ALICE: But we are three here!

THE CAPTAIN: Are you having one, too? Very well, then—three.

ALICE: But where am I to get them? Last evening you invited Kurt to have supper with us, and we didn't have so much as a piece of bread in the house. Kurt has been up all night, watching over you, and hasn't had a bite to eat; he hasn't even had a cup of coffee, because none is left, and our credit is gone.

THE CAPTAIN: *(To Kurt.)* She is angry with me because I didn't die last night. . . .

ALICE: No, because you didn't die twenty-five years ago—because you did not die before I was born.

THE CAPTAIN: *(To Kurt.)* Listen to her! There you see what happens when you bring two persons together in marriage, my dear Kurt! One thing is certain: our marriage was not made in heaven. *(Alice and Kurt exchange meaningful*

48

glances. The Captain gets up and walks toward the doors, Center.) However, you may say what you like, now I am going on duty. *(He puts on an old-fashioned artillery helmet with a plume, girds on his sabre, and then puts on his cloak. Alice and Kurt try vainly to prevent him from going out.)* Out of my way!

(He goes outside.)

ALICE: Yes, go! You always do—always turn tail and beat a retreat when the battle goes against you; and then you let your wife lead you to safety, you drinking-hero, you braggart among braggarts, your archliar! Phew!

KURT: This is a bottomless hell!

ALICE: Oh, but you don't know it all yet. . . .

KURT: Is there still more?

ALICE: Oh, I feel ashamed!

KURT: Where is he going now? And how can he have the strength?

ALICE: You may well ask. Now, of course, he is going over to the non-commissioned officers to thank them for the flowers —and then he will eat and drink with them. And then he'll malign his fellow-officers. . . . If you only knew how many times he has been threatened with dismissal—only regard for his family has kept him from being dismissed. And yet he conceitedly thinks it is out of fear of his superiority. And those poor officers' wives who have taken our part he both hates and slanders.

KURT: I must confess that I applied for this post hoping to find some peace out here by the sea. I knew nothing about your circumstances or the strained relations between you.

ALICE: Poor Kurt! How will you now get something to eat?

KURT: Oh, I can go over to the Doctor's; but how about you? Do let me see about something for you. . . .

ALICE: Don't mention anything to him, however, for then he would kill me.

KURT: *(Looking out through the French windows.)* Look, there he stands on the rampart—the wind whirling about him.

ALICE: What a pity that he behaves the way he does.

KURT: You are both to be pitied. But what can you do about it?

ALICE: I have no idea. We received a stack of bills this morning—but he didn't see those.

KURT: Sometimes it is better not to see. . . .

ALICE: *(At the window.)* His cloak is wide open and the wind is beating on his chest. . . . He evidently wants to die.

KURT: I don't think he does. Only a moment ago, when he felt his life ebbing, he hooked on to me and started to meddle in my personal affairs as though he were about to crawl into me and live my life for me.

ALICE: That is his vampire nature manifesting itself—laying hold of other people's fates, sucking interest out of other people's lives, regulating and managing the affairs of others, because his own life is so completely lacking in interest. And remember, Kurt, never allow him to be part of your family life and let him never meet your friends, for he will steal them from you and monopolize them. He is nothing short of a wizard when it comes to that. And if he were to meet your children, it wouldn't be long before you found them on most intimate terms with him; he would advise them and bring them up according to his ideas and, most important, contrary to yours.

KURT: Alice, tell me—was it he who took my children away from me at the time of the divorce?

ALICE: Now that it is all over—yes, it was he.

KURT: I have suspected it, but wasn't sure. So it *was* he, then!

ALICE: When you—with full confidence in my husband—sent him as peacemaker to your wife, he started a flirtation with her and showed her the trick whereby she obtained the custody of the children.

KURT: Oh God! God in heaven!

ALICE: There you have another side of him you didn't know. *(Silence.)*

KURT: Can you imagine that last night, when he thought he was dying, he—he made me promise to look after his children?

ALICE: You are not going to take out your revenge on my children?

KURT: By keeping my promise? Yes! I shall look after your children.

ALICE: You couldn't take a more stinging revenge, for there is nothing he abhors more than nobility of mind, and magnanimity.

KURT: In that case, I may consider myself revenged—without taking it.

ALICE: I take a passionate delight in revenge as a means of justice, and I revel in seeing evil get its just punishment.

KURT: You are still harping on that!

ALICE: And always shall! If you should ever hear me say I forgave, or loved, an enemy, I would be a hypocrite.

KURT: Alice—there are times when it may be a duty not to tell everything, not to see everything. This is what we call tolerance, or forbearance. It is something we all need.

ALICE: Not I! My life is an open book, and I have always played the game fairly.

KURT: That's saying a good deal.

ALICE: Yet not enough. What I have suffered innocently because of this man—whom I have never loved. . . .

KURT: Why did you marry him?

ALICE: That is the question.—Because he took me—seduced me. . . . I don't know . . . and then I wanted to advance myself socially. . . .

KURT: And so you gave up your stage career.

ALICE: Which he looked down upon. . . . But, you see, he deceived me. He held out to me the alluring prospect of a genial, cheerful life—a beautiful home—and he turned out to be over head and ears in debt. The only gold he possessed was the uniform buttons—and even they were mere imitation. He tricked me!

KURT: Wait a moment! When a young man falls in love, he looks to the future with great expectations. . . . That his hopes are not always realized, we must not hold against him. I myself have the same kind of deceit on my conscience—

51

yet I do not consider myself perfidious or lacking in integrity. *(To Alice, who is looking out of the French windows.)* What do you see out there on the rampart?

ALICE: I am looking to see if he has fallen.

KURT: Has he fallen?

ALICE: No, unfortunately. He always fools me.

KURT: Well, I'm going over to the Doctor now, and to the judge advocate.

ALICE: *(Seating herself by the window.)* Yes, you do that, Kurt dear. I'll wait here. That's something I have learned—to wait. . . .

END OF ACT I

ACT II   SCENE 1

The setting is the same as in Act I.

It is daylight—The sentry on guard duty at the battery paces back and forth.

Alice is seated in the armchair, left. She has now turned gray. Kurt enters from the right, after having first knocked.

KURT: How-do-you-do, Alice?

ALICE: How-do-you-do, Kurt dear. Sit down.

KURT: *(Seating himself in the armchair, right.)* The steamboat is just arriving.

ALICE: Then I know what we can expect, if he is on board.

KURT: Yes, he's on board—I saw his helmet gleaming in the sun.—What has he been doing in the city?

ALICE: I have a good idea of that. Because he was dressed in parade uniform, he must have gone to see the Colonel; and since he wore a pair of fresh gloves, he must have paid some visits in town.

KURT: Did you notice how quiet he was all day yesterday? Ever since he gave up drinking, and eats with moderation, he is a different person: quiet, reserved, and considerate.

ALICE: I know the symptoms! If that man had always stayed sober, he would have been a menace to humanity. Perhaps it is fortunate that he has made himself ridiculous, and so innocuous through his drinking.

KURT: The spirits in the bottle have punished him!—But have you noticed that since death has put its mark on him, he has acquired a semblance of sublime dignity. It is not impossible that he—with the recently awakened thought of immortality germinating in him—has come to have a different view of life.

ALICE: You are deceiving yourself! His intentions are evil. And do not believe him, for he lies deliberately; and he knows the art of intrigue as no one.

KURT: *(Regarding Alice.)* Alice! What do I see? In these two nights your hair has turned gray.

ALICE: No, my friend, it's been gray for years. But now that my husband is practically dead for me, I have stopped tinting. Walled in for twenty-five years in a prison!—Do you know that this fort was used as a prison in olden days?

KURT: A prison. . . . I can tell from the look of the walls.

ALICE: And from my complexion! Even the children developed prison-pallor in this house.

KURT: I can't imagine little children prattling within these walls.

ALICE: You seldom heard any prattling. And the two who died, they faded away for lack of light.

KURT: What do you think will happen next?

ALICE: The decisive attack on us two. When you read that telegram from Judith, I saw a glimmer in his eye—an expression I know only too well. It was, of course, intended for her, but —as you know—she is sacred to him, and so he vented his ire on you instead.

KURT: What can he do to me, do you think?

ALICE: That's hard to say. But he has a phenomenal talent— in addition to luck—for snooping out other people's secrets. And you couldn't have helped noticing how he, all through the day, almost lived in your quarantine station—how he gobbled up interest in life from you—and how he devoured your children alive. . . . I know him too well, you see, this man-eater! His own life is almost at an end—practically gone. . . .

KURT: I have the same feeling—that he is already on the other side. . . . His face sort of phosphoresces—as if he were in a state of dissolution—and his eyes glimmer and flicker like will-o'-the-wisps over marsh and grave.—Here he comes. . . . Tell me—has it ever occurred to you that he might be jealous?

54

ALICE: Oh no, he is much too conceited for that! "Show me a man of whom I would have to be jealous!" Those are his own words.

KURT: So much the better; even his faults can be used to our advantage, then.—Shall I get up and greet him—what do you think?

ALICE: No, be discourteous to him, or he will think we are deceitful. And when he starts telling his lies, act as though you believed him. I am an expert at translating them, and —with the aid of my dictionary—I always manage to get at the truth. . . . I sense something sinister is afoot—but, Kurt, don't lose your equanimity. In the long struggle between us, my one advantage has been the fact that I was always sober and therefore never lost my self-control. Whiskey was his downfall. Well, now we'll see. . . .

> (The Captain enters from the right, dressed in parade uniform with helmet, cloak and white gloves. He is calm, but pale and holloweyed, and carries himself with dignity. As he walks, he stumbles, and seats himself at the extreme left, at a distance from Kurt and Alice. Throughout the ensuing scene he rests his sabre between his knees.)

THE CAPTAIN: Howdoyoudo.—Pardon me for sitting down like this, but I am a little tired.

ALICE AND KURT: Howdoyoudo. And welcome back.

ALICE: How are you feeling?

THE CAPTAIN: Splendidly. But a little tired.

ALICE: What news from the city?

THE CAPTAIN: Oh, one thing and another. I saw the doctor, among others, and he said nothing was wrong with me and that I could live another twenty years if I took care of myself.

ALICE: (To Kurt, in a low tone of voice.) Now he is lying. (To the Captain.) That's good to hear, Edgar dear.

THE CAPTAIN: Yes, it was.

> (There is a silence, during which the Captain keeps

looking at Alice and Kurt as if he were imploring them to say something.)

ALICE: *(To Kurt.)* Don't say anything—let him speak first; then he'll show his cards.

THE CAPTAIN: *(To Alice.)* Did you say something?

ALICE: No, I didn't say anything.

THE CAPTAIN: *(Deliberately.)* Listen, Kurt. . . .

ALICE: *(To Kurt.)* Here it comes. You'll see. . . .

THE CAPTAIN: I—I have been in the city, as you know. . . . *(Kurt nods an acknowledgment.)* And—h'm—I—I made some acquaintances . . . among others, with a young cadet officer . . . *(Lingering.)* . . . in the artillery. *(There is a pause, during which Kurt is beginning to show uneasiness.)* And since . . . since we are particularly in need of cadet officers here, I am arranging with the Colonel to have him assigned here. . . . That ought to gratify you, especially when I inform you that the young man—is—your own son.

ALICE: *(To Kurt.)* There you see—the vampire!

KURT: Under ordinary circumstances this would be pleasing news to a father, but in my case it is only distressing.

THE CAPTAIN: I don't see why it should be.

KURT: You don't need to—it's enough that I oppose it.

THE CAPTAIN: So-o, that's how you feel about it, eh? Then I must tell you that the young man has already been ordered to report here and that from now on he is under my command.

KURT: In that case, I shall force him to apply for transfer to another regiment.

THE CAPTAIN: You can't do that—you have no rights over your son.

KURT: Haven't I?

THE CAPTAIN: No, the Court awarded all rights to the mother.

KURT: Then I'll get in touch with her.

THE CAPTAIN: You don't need to.

KURT: Don't need to?

THE CAPTAIN: No, for I have already seen her. Cha!

(Kurt gets up but sinks back into his chair.)

ALICE: *(To Kurt.)* This is his death-doom!

KURT: Yes, he is a man-eater! That's what he is!

THE CAPTAIN: Well, that was that! *(Facing Alice and Kurt.)* Did you say anything, eh?

ALICE: No. Don't you hear well?

THE CAPTAIN: No—not too well—not always. . . . But if you will come a little closer, I have something to tell you—in strictest confidence. . . .

ALICE: No need for that! And it may be of advantage to both parties to have a witness.

THE CAPTAIN: You are quite right—it's always a good thing to have witnesses. . . . But, first of all, did you receive the will —is it ready?

ALICE: *(Hands him a document.)* The Judge Advocate has drawn it up himself.

THE CAPTAIN: In your favor. Good. *(He glances over the document, tears it carefully into strips, which he throws on the floor.)* That was that! Cha!

ALICE: *(To Kurt.)* Have you ever seen a human creature like him?

KURT: He is not human!

THE CAPTAIN: Oh yes—there was something I wanted to say to Alice. . . .

ALICE: *(Uneasily, yet somewhat ironically.)* By all means!

THE CAPTAIN: *(Cool and unruffled as before.)* On account of your frequently expressed desire to put an end to this miserable life, this unhappy marriage, and because of the heartlessness with which you have treated your husband and children, and the carelessness you have displayed in handling the household affairs, I have now—during my trip to the city—filed an application for divorce in the Municipal Court.

ALICE: So-o? And on what grounds?

THE CAPTAIN: *(Cooly as before.)* Besides the grounds I just mentioned, I have others of a purely personal nature. As I have now learned that I can expect to live another twenty years,

57

I am thinking of exchanging this miserable marriage of ours for one that suits me better and is more becoming to my rank, and to join my destiny with that of some woman who can bring youth and, let us say, a semblance of beauty into the home, in addition to devotion.

ALICE: *(Takes off her wedding ring and throws it at the Captain.)* There you have my answer!

THE CAPTAIN: *(Picks up the ring and pockets it in his waistcoat.)* She threw away her wedding ring. The witness will please note this!

ALICE: *(Rises in agitation.)* So it is your intention to throw me out and put another woman in my place?

THE CAPTAIN: Cha!

ALICE: If that's the case, then let us not mince words! Cousin Kurt, this man is guilty of attempted murder of his wife!

KURT: Murder?

ALICE: Yes—he pushed me into the sea!

THE CAPTAIN: *Without* witnesses!

ALICE: Another lie! Judith saw it!

THE CAPTAIN: What if she did!

ALICE: She can testify!

THE CAPTAIN: Oh no, she can't. She saw nothing, she says.

ALICE: You have taught her to lie.

THE CAPTAIN: I didn't have to—you taught her that.

ALICE: Have you seen Judith?

THE CAPTAIN: Cha!

ALICE: Oh God! Oh God!

THE CAPTAIN: The fortress surrenders. The enemy will be granted ten minutes to withdraw and march off at liberty. *(He puts his watch on the table.)* Ten minutes! The time is ticking!

> *(He remains standing; his hand suddenly goes to his head.)*

ALICE: *(Goes to him and grasps him by the arm.)* What's the matter?

THE CAPTAIN: I don't know. . . .

ALICE: Is there anything I can bring you? Would you like something to drink?

THE CAPTAIN: Whiskey? No—I don't want to die!—So it's you! *(He pulls himself together and straightens up.)* Don't touch me!—Ten minutes—or the garrison will be struck down! *(With partly drawn sabre.)* Ten minutes!
(He goes out, rear.)

KURT: What specimen of man is this?

ALICE: He's a demon—not a human being!

KURT: What does he want of my son?

ALICE: He wants him as a hostage so that he can dominate you; his plan is to isolate you from the authorities on the island. —Do you know that the natives here call this island "the little hell"?

KURT: I hadn't heard that. . . . Alice, you are the first woman to stir me to compassion. . . . All the others I felt deserved their fate.

ALICE: Don't desert me now! Don't leave me—he would strike me. . . . He has threatened to do that for twenty-five years —and in the presence of the children—he has pushed me into the sea. . . .

KURT: When I heard that, I had no more use for the man! I came here without harboring any rankling over his past humiliations. I even forgave him after you had told me that it was he who was responsible for my children being taken from me. I forgave him because he was ill and dying; but when he now wants to take my son from me—he must die! It is either he—or I!

ALICE: You are right! Don't give up the fortress. . . . Even if we have to blow it up, and him with it, with us two keeping him company. I'll handle the powder-keg!

KURT: When I came here, I had no rancor in me, yet I felt like leaving, when I sensed that your hate was contaminating me. But now I feel an irrepressible urge to hate this man as deeply as I have always hated all evilness.—What can we do now?

ALICE: I have learned the tactics from him: drum up his enemies and let us find allies.

KURT: To think that he could ferret out my wife! Why couldn't
these two have met a generation ago! There would have
been conflict enough to make the earth tremble!

ALICE: But now that their two souls have met . . . they must
be torn apart! I believe I know where he is most vulnerable
—I have long had my suspicions. . . .

KURT: Who is his most obdurate enemy on the island?

ALICE: The ordinance officer.

KURT: Is he an honorable man?

ALICE: Yes, he is. And he knows what I—what I know, too. He
knows what intrigues the sergeant major and the Captain
have been up to.

KURT: What have they been up to? You don't mean that. . . .

ALICE: Embezzlement!

KURT: That is disgraceful!—No, I refuse to have anything to
do with that!

ALICE: Ha, ha! You mean you refuse to strike down an enemy?

KURT: There was a time when I could. I can't any more.

ALICE: Why?

KURT: Because I have learned—that in the end justice prevails.

ALICE: But in the meantime your son will be taken from you!
Look at my gray hair—if you feel it, you will see it is still
thick!—He intends to marry another, and then I am free—to
do the same.—I'll be free again! And in ten minutes he shall
be under arrest—down below—in the dungeon. . . . *(She
stamps on the floor.)* . . . down in the dungeon . . . and I
shall dance on his head—I shall dance to the tune of 'The
Entry of the Boyars'. . . . *(She takes a few steps, dancing with
her hands on her hips.)* Hahahaha! I shall hammer on the
piano so that he will hear! *(She bangs on the piano.)* Oh!
The fortress gates shall open and the sentry with drawn
sabre will no longer be guarding me, but him . . . Meli-tam-
tam-ta-meli-tah-lee-ah-li! He shall be guarding him—him
—him!

60

KURT: *(Looking at her, bewitched.)* Alice, Are you, too, a demon?

ALICE: *(Jumps up on a chair and pulls down the laurel wreaths.)* I am going to take these with me when I march off. . . . The laurels of triumph with their fluttering ribbons. . . . A trifle dusty, but eternally green—like my youth. . . . I am not so old, am I, Kurt?

KURT: *(His eyes gleaming.)* You are a demon!

ALICE: In 'little hell'!—And now I am going to get dressed . . . *(She takes down her hair.)* I'll be ready in two minutes—it will take me two minutes to get to the ordinance officer—and then . . . then up goes the fortress! Up in the air!

KURT: *(As before.)* You are a demon!

ALICE: You used to call me that when we were children also. Do you remember when we were children and said we were engaged? Do you? *(She laughs.)* You were bashful, as always.

KURT: *(In a serious tone.)* Alice!

ALICE: Yes, you were—and it was becoming to you. You know, there are rude women who like timid, bashful men—just as you may find shy men who are partial to rude, overpowering women.—I imagine you sort of liked me then? Didn't you?

KURT: I don't know—I am lost. . . .

ALICE: You are not lost—you are with me, an actress with uninhibited views, but who nonetheless is an exemplary woman. Yes, indeed! And now I am free—free—free! Now—if you will turn your back to me, I'll just change this shirtwaist. . . .

(She unbuttons her shirtwaist. Kurt rushes up to her and embraces her, then lifts her high in the air. Biting her neck, he causes her to cry out. Then he throws her down on the sofa and runs out, right.)

END OF SCENE 1

ACT II   SCENE 2

The same setting. It is now evening.

The sentry at the battery emplacements can still be observed through the French window panes. The laurel wreaths are hung over the arms of a chair. The ceiling lamp is lighted. Faint music is heard from the outside. The Captain, pale and hollow-eyed, his hair iron-gray, is seated at the writing table, playing solitaire. He is wearing spectacles, and is dressed in a worn fatigue uniform and riding boots.

The entr'acte music continues after the rise of the curtain until the next character appears on the stage.

The Captain lays out the cards; occasionally he gives a start, his face twitching, looks up and listens anxiously.

He seems to have difficulty making the cards come out, grows impatient, and puts away the deck, walks over to the windows on the right, opens the door and flings the pack of cards outside. He leaves the door open; and one can hear it rattling on its hinges.

He goes over to the cabinet, but is frightened by the sound of the creaking, rattling door; he turns to see what causes the sound, and then takes out three square, dark-colored whiskey bottles, regards them hesitatingly and throws them out of the door. Similarly he takes out several boxes of cigars, opens one and sniffs of it, then throws them all outside.

This done, he takes off his spectacles, wipes them and puts them on again to see whether they improve his sight; and then they are tossed out the same way as the other things. He stumbles against the furniture as if half-blind and lights the six candles in the candelabrum on the chest of drawers. When he notices the laurel wreaths on the armchair, he snatches them up and is about to throw them out of the window also, but changes his mind and walks to the piano. He takes off the piano cover, folds it carefully round the wreaths, fastening the corners together with pins which he picks up on the writing table; and then he places them on a chair. After that, he goes back to the piano, hammers on the keys with his fist, slams down the lid and locks it, whereupon he throws the key out of the French window. He then lights the candles on the piano, walks over to the whatnot, takes his wife's photograph from it, gazes at it and tears it into pieces, which he scatters on the floor. The door shakes and rattles, and again he is frightened.

Having regained his poise, he takes the portraits of his son and daughter, gives them a fleeting kiss and puts them in his breast pocket. The rest of the portraits he sweeps off with his elbow and, with his boot, kicks them into a pile on the floor.

Wearied, he then sits down at the writing table, his hand going to his heart. He lights the reading lamp, sighs, and stares into space as if he were having a horrible vision. He rises and goes over to the bureau-desk, opens the lid and takes out a bundle of letters, tied with a blue silk ribbon, and throws it into the stove, after which he closes the lid of the bureau-desk.

The telegraph apparatus clicks once, after which there is silence. The Captain shrinks in deadly terror and remains standing, clutching at his heart, and listening. As there is no further sound from the apparatus, he turns his ear in the direction of the door on the right and then goes over and opens it, takes a step across the threshold and comes back, carrying on his arm a cat, which he strokes. Then he goes out, left, and the music ceases.

> *(Alice enters from the rear, dressed in a walking suit, with hat and gloves; her hair is now black. She looks about and is surprised to see all the lights lit.—Kurt enters from the right; he seems nervous.)*

ALICE: It looks like Christmas Eve in here.

KURT: Well?

ALICE: *(Offers him her hand to kiss.)* Thank me! *(Kurt kisses her hand reluctantly.)* Six witnesses, four of whom are completely dependable. The complaint has been entered and the answer will be coming here by telegraph—right here in the prison.

KURT: Yes, I see. . . .

ALICE: Instead of saying 'yes, I see!' say 'thank you.'

KURT: Why has he lighted all the candles?

ALICE: Because he is afraid of the dark.—Look at the telegraph apparatus—doesn't it look like the handle of a coffee grinder? I grind, I grind—and the beans crackle and crack—as when you pull teeth. . . .

KURT: What has he done to the room here?

ALICE: It looks as if he were about to move. (*With a gesture toward below.*) Down there—there is where you are moving. . . .

KURT: Don't, Alice, don't! I think it is sad. He was, after all, my boyhood friend, and many a time when I was in dire need, he helped me out. . . . I feel pity for him.

ALICE: What about me? I have done nothing to hurt him—and I gave up my career for this monster!

KURT: How about your career? Was it so very brilliant?

ALICE: (*Enraged.*) What was that you said? Do you realize who I am—what I was?

KURT: Now, now. . . .

ALICE: Are you, too, going to start—so soon?

KURT: So soon?

(*Alice throws her arms round Kurt's neck and kisses him. He lifts her in his arms and bites her neck; she gives a shriek.*)

ALICE: You are biting me. . . .

KURT: (*Beside himself.*) Yes, I want to bite your flesh and suck your blood like a lynx! You have roused the beast in me—the beast which I have tried for years to conquer by privation and mortification. I came out here, and at first I believed myself to be better than you; but now I am more miserable than either of you. Since I came here and saw you—saw you in all your horrible nakedness, my vision warped by pas-

64

sion, I have learned to know the awesome power of evil. The ugly becomes beautiful; what is good turns ugly and despicable. . . . Come here, I want to suffocate you—with a kiss. . . .

(He embraces her.)

ALICE: *(Holding out her left arm.)* Do you see the imprint of the shackles that you release me from? I was the thrall, the bond-woman—and now I am free. . . .

KURT: But I shall bind you. . . .

ALICE: You?

KURT: Yes, I!

ALICE: I thought for a moment you were. . . .

KURT: A pietist?

ALICE: Yes, you kept prating about the Fall. . . .

KURT: Did I?

ALICE: And I thought you had come here to preach. . . .

KURT: Did you?—In an hour we shall be in the city and then you will find out if I'm a preacher. . . .

ALICE: And we'll go to the theatre in the evening, just to show ourselves. You understand, if *I* leave *him*, the shame will be his. You understand, don't you?

KURT: I am beginning to. . . . Imprisonment alone is not enough. . . .

ALICE: No, it is not! He must be shamed, too!

KURT: A curious world! *You* commit the shameful act, and *he* has to bear the shame of it!

ALICE: As long as the world is so stupid!

KURT: It is as if these prison walls had absorbed all the wickedness and depravity of the criminals; merely by breathing the air here, one is contaminated. You, I suppose, were thinking about theatre and supper; I was thinking about my son.

ALICE: *(Strikes him across the mouth with her glove.)* Old fogey! *(Kurt raises his hand to box her ears. Alice shrinks back.)* Tout beau!

KURT: Forgive me!

ALICE: On your knees, then! *(Kurt kneels.)* And on your face!

65

(Kurt bends to the floor.) Kiss my foot! *(Kurt does so.)* And never again! Now get up!

KURT: *(Rises.)* What have I come to? Where am I?

ALICE: You know very well.

KURT: *(Glancing about in horror.)* I would almost think that. . . .

> *(The Captain enters from the left; he is leaning on a walking stick and looks miserable.)*

THE CAPTAIN: *(To Alice.)* Will you let me speak with Kurt? Alone.

ALICE: Is it about our departure and the safe conduct?

THE CAPTAIN: *(Seating himself at the sewing table.)* Kurt! Will you be good enough to sit down here with me for a moment? And will you, Alice, let us have one moment of—of peace?

ALICE: *(To the Captain.)* What are you up to now? New signals? *(To Kurt.)* Please be seated. *(Kurt sits down reluctantly.)* And listen to words of wisdom, and of age! *(Pointing to the telegraph apparatus.)* If a message should come—then let me know.

> *(She goes out, right.)*

THE CAPTAIN: *(After a pause, with dignity.)* Can you understand a human destiny like mine, like ours? Can you?

KURT: No—not any more than I can understand my own.

THE CAPTAIN: What meaning is there to all this turmoil, chaos and confusion?

KURT: In my more sanguine moments I have felt its meaning to be that we were not to know, or question, the meaning of life, but simply be submissive.

THE CAPTAIN: Be submissive! With no fixed extraneous point, I can't be submissive.

KURT: Quite correct. But you, as a mathematician, ought to be able to find that unknown point, when you have several given ones.

THE CAPTAIN: I have searched for it, but—I haven't found it.

KURT: Then you have made some mistake in your calculations. Start all over again!

THE CAPTAIN: I'll do that.—Tell me, from where did you get your resignation, your humility?

KURT: I haven't any left. Don't overestimate me.

THE CAPTAIN: As you may have noticed, I have summed up the art of living this way: eradicate—rub out! And keep going! In other words: obliterate! Early in life I made myself a sack, into which I crammed all my humiliations; and when it was brimful, I tossed it into the sea.—I don't believe any man has suffered so many humiliations as I have. But when I blotted them out, and kept on going, they ceased to exist.

KURT: I have noticed how you have shaped not only your own life but life about you, out of your poetic imagination.

THE CAPTAIN: How should I have been able to live otherwise? How could I have endured life?

(He clutches at his heart.)

KURT: How are you feeling?

THE CAPTAIN: Poorly. *(Silence.)* But then comes the moment when your imagination—when your poetic imagination, as you call it, runs out—when you can no longer create. And *then* you find yourself face to face with reality in all its nakedness.—That is what is so terrifying! *(He suddenly begins to speak like an old man, with tears in his voice and drooping chin.)* You see, my dear friend. . . . *(He controls himself and reverts to his usual manner of speech.)* I beg your pardon! . . . When I was in the city I consulted the doctor there, and he said. . . . *(Again with tears in his voice.)* . . . he said that my health was broken and . . . *(In his ordinary voice.)* and that I hadn't long to live.

KURT: He said that?

THE CAPTAIN: Yes, that's what he said.

KURT: So it wasn't true, then . . . ?

THE CAPTAIN: What?—Oh, I see . . . No—it wasn't true.

(Silence.)

KURT: Then the other thing you mentioned wasn't true either?

THE CAPTAIN: What other thing do you mean, Kurt?

KURT: What you said about my son being ordered here as cadet officer.

67

THE CAPTAIN: I have never heard a word about that.

KURT: You know, your propensity for erasing your own misdeeds is unbounded.

THE CAPTAIN: I don't know what you are talking about, my dear Kurt.

KURT: In that case, you are at the end of the road.

THE CAPTAIN: Yes—there isn't *much* left of me.

KURT: And I suppose you haven't filed a petition for divorce either—an action that would cast such a disgrace upon your wife?

THE CAPTAIN: Divorce, did you say?—No, I know nothing about that.

KURT: *(Getting up.)* Then—will you admit that you have been lying?

THE CAPTAIN: My dear Kurt, you use such strong words. We have to be tolerant, Kurt,—all of us.

KURT: You have come to realize that, have you?

THE CAPTAIN: *(Resolutely, in a clear voice.)* Yes, I have come to that conclusion. Will you therefore forgive me, Kurt? Forgive everything?

KURT: There you spoke like a man.—But I have nothing to forgive you. And I am not the man you always believed me to be—not any longer. And least of all am I worthy of receiving your confessions.

THE CAPTAIN: *(In a clear voice.)* Life for me has been so strange—so hostile, so vile—ever since my childhood . . . and people so mean, and as a consequence I grew to be mean also. *(Kurt paces about uneasily and keeps glancing at the telegraph apparatus.)* What are you looking at?

KURT: Can a telegraph set be turned off?

THE CAPTAIN: No, not very well.

KURT: *(With increasing uneasiness.)* Who is Östberg, the sergeant major?

THE CAPTAIN: He is a very honest fellow. A bit of a businessman, however.

KURT: And who is the ordinance officer?

THE CAPTAIN: Although he is my enemy, I have nothing bad to say about him.

KURT: *(Noticing the light from a lantern in motion, outside the French windows.)* What are they doing with that lantern out by the battery?

THE CAPTAIN: You see a lantern there?

KURT: Yes—and people moving about. . . .

THE CAPTAIN: I assume it's what we call a detail.

KURT: And what's that?

THE CAPTAIN: A corporal and a few men. Probably some poor fellow they are taking to jail.

KURT: Oh!

(There is a pause.)

THE CAPTAIN: Well, now that you know Alice—what do you think of her?

KURT: I can't answer that. . . . I don't understand people in the least. She is as much a riddle to me as you are, not to mention myself. You see, I am approaching the age when sensible people acknowledge that they know nothing, understand nothing. But whenever I see anything being done, I want to know the reason for it.—Just why did you push her into the water?

THE CAPTAIN: I don't know. She was standing there on the pier, and on the spur of the moment it seemed quite natural to me that she ought to be in the water.

KURT: Didn't you ever feel sorry about it?

THE CAPTAIN: Never!

KURT: That is extraordinary!

THE CAPTAIN: Yes, it really is. It is so weird that I can't believe I ever did such a nefarious deed.

KURT: Hasn't it occurred to you that she might seek revenge?

THE CAPTAIN: I think she has taken sufficient revenge on me—and I find that just as natural.

KURT: What has made you so cynically resigned suddenly?

THE CAPTAIN: Since I looked death in the eye, I have come to view life differently. Tell me, Kurt—if you were to judge

69

between Alice and me—who would you say was in the right?

KURT: Neither. But for both of you I have pity—endless pity—perhaps a little more for you.

THE CAPTAIN: Give me your hand, Kurt!

KURT: *(Putting one hand on the Captain's shoulder he extends the other to him.)* My old friend!

ALICE: *(Carrying a parasol, she enters from the right.)* Well, well, how intimate we've become! Oh well, such is friendship! Hasn't any message come yet?

KURT: *(Coldly.)* No.

ALICE: This waiting makes me impatient; and when I become impatient I expedite matters promptly.—Now, Kurt, see me fire the final shot at him—and that will be the end of him. . . . First, I load—I know the manual, his famous rifle manual that never sold even five thousand copies—and now I take aim. . . . *(She aims her parasol at him.)* How is your new wife? Your young wife—the beautiful one? You don't know! But I know how my lover is! *(She puts her arms round Kurt's neck and kisses him. He pushes her away.)* He is in excellent health, but he has not got over his bashfulness. *(To the Captain.)* You miserable creature, whom I have never loved! You never realized how I led you by the nose, because you were too conceited to be jealous!

> *(The Captain draws his sabre and rushes toward her threateningly. Slashing right and left he, however, only damages the furniture.)*

ALICE: *(Screaming.)* Help! Help!

> *(Kurt stands motionless. The Captain collapses and falls to the floor, still clutching the sabre.)*

THE CAPTAIN: Judith! Avenge me, Judith!

ALICE: Hurrah! He is dead!

> *(Kurt withdraws toward the rear door.)*

THE CAPTAIN: *(Struggling to his feet.)* Not yet!

> *(He puts his sabre back in the scabbard and goes to sit down in the armchair by the sewing-table.)*

ALICE: *(Going up to Kurt.)* Now I am ready—to come with you!

KURT: *(Pushes her away so that she falls to her knees.)* Go back to the depths from where you come!—Goodbye—for ever!
    (He starts to leave.)

THE CAPTAIN: Don't leave, Kurt! She will kill me!
    (Kurt leaves.)

ALICE: Kurt! Do not leave me—don't desert me!

KURT: Goodbye!

ALICE: *(Suddenly changing her attitude.)* What a scoundrel! There is a friend for you!

THE CAPTAIN: *(Gently.)* Forgive me, Alice, and come over to me. Quickly!

ALICE: *(To the Captain.)* He is the worst scoundrel, the worst hypocrite I have ever met in all my life! No matter what you may say—*you* are a man!

THE CAPTAIN: Alice, listen to me. . . . I am not going to live much longer. . . .

ALICE: So-o?

THE CAPTAIN: The doctor told me.

ALICE: Then what you said before was untrue?

THE CAPTAIN: Yes.

ALICE: *(Beside herself.)* Oh! What have I done!

THE CAPTAIN: There is nothing that can't be helped.

ALICE: No, no—this is beyond all help!

THE CAPTAIN: Nothing is beyond help if you blot it out, rub it out—and then continue on. . . .

ALICE: But the telegraph message! . . .

THE CAPTAIN: Which message?

ALICE: *(Falls on her knees before the Captain.)* Are we rejected —doomed? Was this meant to happen? I have blown my life to pieces—destroyed us both! Why did you have to lie? And why did this man have to come and tempt me?—We are lost! Had you been noble and generous of heart, everything might have been forgiven.

THE CAPTAIN: What is there that cannot be forgiven? Have you ever done anything that I have not forgiven?

ALICE: Oh—but this is unforgivable!

THE CAPTAIN: I have no idea what it is, although I know how clever you are when it comes to inventing infamy and trickery.

ALICE: Oh, if I could only get out of this. If I could . . . if I could—I would care for you, Edgar—I would love you. . . .

THE CAPTAIN: Now, listen to me. . . . What is it all about?

ALICE: Do you think anyone can help us—no! No one—no one in this world!

THE CAPTAIN: If not in this world—then who?

ALICE: *(Looking at him.)* I don't know.—Oh heavens! What will become of the children—with our name disgraced?

THE CAPTAIN: Have you brought dishonor to our name?

ALICE: Not I! Not I!—They will have to leave school! And when they go out into the world, they will be as lonely and alone as we are—and as mean!— *(Suddenly struck by a thought.)* I am just beginning to realize now you didn't see Judith, either!

THE CAPTAIN: No, but forget about that!

(The telegraph receiver starts to click. Alice leaps to her feet.)

ALICE: *(Screaming.)* Here comes the deathblow! *(To the Captain.)* Don't listen to it!

THE CAPTAIN: *(Calmly.)* I shan't listen, my dear child, you needn't get excited! *(Alice, over by the apparatus, is seen standing on tiptoe looking out of the window.)*

ALICE: Don't listen! Don't listen!

THE CAPTAIN: *(Covering his ears with his hands.)* I have my ears covered, Alice, my child.

ALICE: *(On her knees, with outstretched hands.)* Oh God! Help us!—The men on detail out there are coming. . . . *(She cries hysterically.)* God in heaven! *(Her lips move as if in silent prayer. The telegraph receiver is still heard, clicking faintly, and a long strip of paper has fallen from it. After another moment it stops clicking.—Alice rises, tears off the paper strip and reads it in silence. Then she casts her eyes heaven-*

ward and walks over to the Captain kissing him on the fore-head.) It is all over! It was nothing!

(She sits down in the other armchair and falls into violent weeping. She wipes the tears off her face with her handkerchief.)

THE CAPTAIN: What are all these secrets you have . . . ?

ALICE: Don't ask me! It is over now!

THE CAPTAIN: As you say, my child.

ALICE: You would never have spoken like this three days ago! —What has come over you?

THE CAPTAIN: You see, my dear—when I fell the first time, I was already on the other side of the grave—in the beyond. What I saw there I have forgotten—but the subconscious memory of it remains. . . .

ALICE: The memory of what?

THE CAPTAIN: Hope—the hope of a better life!

ALICE: A better life?

THE CAPTAIN: Yes—for I have never really thought of this life as the end of life. . . . This life of ours is death itself, or something even worse. . . .

ALICE: And we . . .

THE CAPTAIN: Our destiny is, no doubt, to torment one another—or so it seems. . . .

ALICE: Have we two tormented each other sufficiently, do you think?

THE CAPTAIN: I think we have! And wreaked chaos and destruction. *(He looks about.)* Shall we tidy up the mess we have made? And clean house?

ALICE: *(Rising.)* Yes—if we can. . . .

THE CAPTAIN: *(Looking around the room.)* It will take more than one day. No doubt of that.

ALICE: It might take more than that—many more. . . .

THE CAPTAIN: Let us hope. . . . *(There is a silence.)* *(The Captain seats himself again.)* And so you didn't get away from me this time! On the other hand, you didn't hook me, either! *(Alice seems taken aback.)* Yes, I knew you wanted

73

to put me in prison—but I cross that off. It's erased—I imagine you have done worse things than that. . . . *(Alice is speechless.)* And I am not guilty of any embezzlement either!

ALICE: And now you want me to be your nurse?

THE CAPTAIN: If you so wish.

ALICE: What else is there for me to do?

THE CAPTAIN: I don't know.

ALICE: *(Sits down, listless, agonized.)* These are the torments of eternity! Is there no end to them, then?

THE CAPTAIN: Yes, if we have patience. Perhaps life only begins after death. . . .

ALICE: If it were so!
      (Silence.)

THE CAPTAIN: Do you think of Kurt as a hypocrite?

ALICE: I most certainly do.

THE CAPTAIN: I do not. But everyone who comes in contact with us, becomes tainted, turns evil, and leaves us. Kurt was weak—and evil is strong. *(Pause.)* Just think how banal life of today is! In olden days people fought; today people only shake a fist at you!—I am almost certain that three months from now we shall celebrate our silver wedding and that Kurt will give away the bride—and with the doctor and Gerda, his wife, present as guests. The ordinance officer will give the festal speech, and the sergeant major will be the cheerleader. If I know the Colonel aright, he will invite himself.—Yes, you may laugh—but do you remember Adolph's silver wedding—the fellow in the Riflemen's Corps, you know. . . . The silverbride had to wear her ring on her right hand because the bridegroom, in a moment of tenderness, had cut off her ring finger with his saber. *(Alice suppresses a laugh by putting her handkerchief to her mouth.)* Are you crying?—No, I believe you are laughing!—Yes, my child, we cry one day, and the next we laugh. . . . And don't ask me which is the best for us. . . . I read in a newspaper the other day that a man had been divorced seven times. Finally—at the age of ninety-eight—he remarried his first wife. That's love for you! If life is a serious venture or merely a farce—that is a mystery I can't comprehend. When it plays pranks on us, it can prove to be most painful; and the serious aspect is really the more tranquil and peaceful. . . . But as soon as one finally grows to be serious—then someone suddenly appears to play pranks on you. Take Kurt, for example! . . . Do you want us to celebrate our silver wedding? *(Alice is silent.)* Say that you do!—People will be laughing at us, but what do we care! We'll laugh along with them; or we'll keep a straight face—whichever suits us best.

> *(Alice is silent.)*

ALICE: Well, let's celebrate then.

THE CAPTAIN: *(With a serious mien.)* Hence—the silver wedding! . . . *(He rises.)* Erase—and keep going! And so—let us go on!

END OF PART I

Part Two

Edgar
Alice
Kurt
Allan, son of Kurt
Judith, Edgar's daughter
The Lieutenant

The Setting:

An oval drawing-room in white and gold.

Set into the rear wall and occupying almost the whole breadth of it, a row of French windows, which stand open and reveal a terrace with a stone balustrade. On this are placed delicately blue majolica jardinières with petunias and scarlet geraniums.

The terrace serves as a public walk. Beyond the terrace can be seen the shore battery emplacements where an artilleryman is on sentry duty, and farther in the background is discerned the open sea.

In the drawing-room, on the left, stands a sofa, with gilt frame, a table and chairs; on the right is a grand piano, a writing table and a fireplace with mantelpiece. An American easy chair stands down-stage. At the side of the writing table, a smaller table, beside which stands a floor-lamp of brass for reading.

On the walls are hung a number of old oil paintings.

ACT I   SCENE 1

*Allan is seated at the writing table, struggling with a
mathematical problem. Judith, with her hair hanging
down in a braid, enters from the terrace. She is wearing
a short, summery dress and carries in one hand her hat,
in the other a tennis racket. She stops in the doorway.
Allan, serious of mien and courteous of manner, gets
up from his chair.*

JUDITH: *(Similarly serious, and friendly in manner.)* Why don't
you come and play tennis?

ALLAN: *(Diffidently, struggling with his emotions.)* I have too
much to do.

JUDITH: Didn't you see that I placed my bicycle facing the oak,
and not the other way around?

ALLAN: Yes, I did.

JUDITH: Well, what does that mean?

ALLAN: It means—that you would like me to come and play
tennis with you. . . . But I have my work—I have some problems I must solve, and your father is a pretty hard task-
master. . . .

JUDITH: Do you like my father?

ALLAN: Yes, I do. He takes an interest in all his students.

JUDITH: He takes an interest in everybody and everything. Will
you come?

ALLAN: You must know that I would like to, but I must not.

JUDITH: I'll ask papa to excuse you.

ALLAN: No, don't! It'll only set people talking.

JUDITH: Don't you think I know how to handle him? He'll do
what *I* want.

ALLAN: I suppose that is because you are so insistent and un-
yielding.

JUDITH: That's what you should be, too!

79

ALLAN: I am not a wolf at heart.

JUDITH: No, you belong with the sheep.

ALLAN: I prefer that.

JUDITH: But tell me—why won't you come and play?

ALLAN: You know the reason.

JUDITH: But tell me the reason! . . . The lieutenant. . . .

ALLAN: You don't care the least about me—and you don't enjoy being with the lieutenant unless I am there, too, so that you can see me suffer.

JUDITH: Am I really so cruel? I had no idea I was!

ALLAN: Now you know it!

JUDITH: Then I must make amends, for I don't wish to be cruel—I don't wish to be bad—in your eyes.

ALLAN: You only say that so that you can dominate me. You already have me as your slave, but you are not satisfied with that. The slave has to be tortured and thrown to the wild beasts! You *have* the other one in your clutches—so what do you want with me? Let me go my way, and you go your way!

JUDITH: Are you telling me to go? *(Allan is silent.)* Very well, I'll go then!—Being cousins, we'll meet again, now and then, but I don't intend to bother you. . . . *(Allan seats himself at the writing table and continues wrestling with his problems. Judith does not leave, but instead moves toward him slowly, step by step, coming over to the table, where Allan sits.)* You don't have to worry—I am going immediately. . . . I just want to see what kind of quarters the quarantine master has. *(She looks about.)* White and gold!—A grand piano—a Bechstein—nothing less!—*We* are still living in the fortress tower after papa was pensioned off—the tower where mama spent twenty-five of her years—and we are living there on sufferance at that!—But you—you are rich. . . .

ALLAN: *(Quietly.)* We are not rich.

JUDITH: That's what you say, but you are always dressed in fine clothes. For that matter, whatever you wear is becoming to you.—Did you hear what I said?

ALLAN: *(Submissively.)* I heard.

JUDITH: How can you hear while you are sitting there making calculations, or whatever it is you are doing?

ALLAN: I don't listen with my eyes.

JUDITH: Your eyes, yes. Have you ever looked at them in the mirror?

ALLAN: Go away from me!

JUDITH: You despise me, don't you?

ALLAN: My dear Judith, I give no thought to you, one way or another!

JUDITH: *(Moving still closer to him.)* Archimedes sits occupied with his mathematics while the soldier comes and stabs him to death.

(She rumples his papers with her tennis racket.)

ALLAN: Don't touch my papers!

JUDITH: That's exactly what Archimedes said. I suppose you go about imagining things, don't you? You imagine I can't live without you.

ALLAN: Why can't you leave me alone?

JUDITH: If you would be polite, I would help you with your examination.

ALLAN: You?

JUDITH: Yes, I know the examiners.

ALLAN: *(With severity.)* What if you do?

JUDITH: Haven't you learned to ingratiate yourself with your teachers?

ALLAN: Are you referring to your father and the lieutenant?

JUDITH: And the Colonel!

ALLAN: And so you mean to insinuate that with your help I could slip through without doing my lessons?

JUDITH: You are a bad translator. . . .

ALLAN: . . . of a bad original!

JUDITH: Aren't you ashamed of yourself?

ALLAN: I am—on your account as well as my own! I am ashamed of having even listened to you!—Why don't you run along?

JUDITH: Because I know you really like having me with you.— Oh yes,—for you always find occasion to pass under my window! You always manage to have an errand to do in the city and to take the same boat as I; and you never go sailing unless you have me to look after the fore-sheet.

ALLAN: *(Shyly.)* A young girl shouldn't talk like that!

JUDITH: Do you mean to say that I am a child?

ALLAN: Occasionally you act like a good child; and then again you act like a wicked woman. You seem to have chosen me to be your sheep.

JUDITH: You *are* a sheep, and that's why I want to protect you.

ALLAN: *(Getting up.)* Wolves make bad shepherds. . . . You want to devour me, that's the gist of it, no doubt. You want to palm off your beautiful eyes in exchange for my head.

JUDITH: Oh, you have been looking at my eyes, have you? I scarcely thought you had enough courage for that.

(Allan gathers his papers and is about to go out, left. Judith places herself before the door.)

ALLAN: Out of my way, or I'll. . . .

JUDITH: Or you will—what?

ALLAN: If you were a boy, I would. . . . Bah! But you are nothing but a girl!

JUDITH: And so. . . .

ALLAN: If you had the slightest trace of pride in you, you would have gone after my having practically shown you the door!

JUDITH: I'll repay you for that!

ALLAN: No doubt!

JUDITH: *(In a rage, going to the door.)* I—shall—pay you—back! *(She leaves.)*

KURT: *(Enters from the right.)* Where are you bound for, Allan?

ALLAN: Ah, it's you!

KURT: Who could that be who left in such a temper that even the shrubbery trembled?

ALLAN: It was Judith.

KURT: She is a little impetuous, a little vehement—but she is a nice girl.

ALLAN: Whenever a girl is mean and rude, she is called a nice girl. . . .

KURT: You must not be so severe, Allan.—Aren't you pleased with your new-found relations?

82

ALLAN: I like Uncle Edgar. . . .

KURT: Yes, he has many good sides. And how do you like your other instructors? The lieutenant, for example?

ALLAN: He is so petulant, so capricious. There are times when I think he harbors a secret grudge against me.

KURT: Oh no! You have a habit of imagining things about people, Allan. Stop fretting, and just do what you have to do —do the correct thing, and leave others to take care of their own affairs.

ALLAN: That's what I do, but I am never left alone. They draw you in—just like the squid down at the Jetty; they don't bite, but they stir up a whirlpool that sucks you in. . . .

KURT: (Gently.) I have a feeling that you are inclined to be morose and moody, Allan. Don't you feel happy being here with me? Is there anything you miss?

ALLAN: I have never enjoyed myself anywhere as much—but . . . there is something here that suffocates me. . . .

KURT: Here—by the sea? Don't you like the sea?

ALLAN: Yes, the open sea! But along the shores here there are cuttle-fish, seaweed in whicn you get entangled, jellyfish, sea-nettle—or whatever it is called.

KURT: You ought not to stay indoors so much. Go out and play tennis.

ALLAN: I get no fun out of it.

KURT: I suppose you are angry with Judith.

ALLAN: Judith?

KURT: You are so choosy about those you associate with. That we can't be, for then we'll be left to ourselves.

ALLAN: I am not fussy, but—I feel as if I were at the bottom of a pile of wood—having to wait my turn to be cast on the fire. All the weight from above keeps pressing on me—pressing on me. . . .

KURT: Be patient—your turn will come—the pile will diminish. . . .

ALLAN: Yes, but it takes so long, so long. . . . Oh! And meantime I have to stay here and grow mouldy. . . .

KURT: To be young is no frolic. And yet you are envied.

ALLAN: Are we? Would you like to change place with me?

KURT: No, thanks.

ALLAN: Do you know what I find hardest to take? Having to keep silent when old people sit and talk twaddle and knowing that I know more about the subject they are discussing than they do. And still have to keep my mouth shut! You'll forgive me, but I don't include *you* among these old people, of course.

KURT: And why not?

ALLAN: Perhaps because we are only just now getting acquainted with each other?

KURT: And because . . . because you have now come to have a different picture of me?

ALLAN: Yes.

KURT: I suppose that during the years we were separated, you didn't always have the friendliest feelings toward me?

ALLAN: No.

KURT: Did you ever see a portrait of me?

ALLAN: Only once—and that was anything but favorable.

KURT: Old-looking, eh?

ALLAN: Yes.

KURT: Ten years ago my hair turned gray, overnight; but—without my doing anything about it—it has come back to its natural color.—Let us talk about something else. . . . Look, there comes your aunt—my cousin. How do you like her?

ALLAN: I prefer not to say.

KURT: Then I shan't press you.

> *(Alice enters. She carries a parasol and is dressed in a very light-colored tailored summer suit.)*

ALICE: Good morning, Kurt.

> *(She indicates by a look that she would like to be alone with Kurt.)*

KURT: *(To Allan.)* We'd like to be alone, Allan.

> *(Allan goes out, left. Alice sits down on the sofa, right. Kurts seats himself on a chair beside her.)*

ALICE: *(Embarrassed.)* Edgar will be here any moment, so don't let it upset you.

84

KURT: Why should it?

ALICE: You—with your strict sense of honor and your correct behavior. . . .

KURT: As regards myself, yes.

ALICE: Exactly! I forgot myself one time when I thought you had come to deliver me—but you kept your self-control—and so there is no reason why we should not forget—what never was. . . .

KURT: Then, let us forget it.

ALICE: However, I don't think that *he* has forgotten.

KURT: Are you alluding to the heart attack he had that night when he collapsed—and when you gloated too prematurely, in the belief that he was dead?

ALICE: Yes. And now that he has recovered, after giving up drinking, he has learned to keep his mouth shut—and now he is abominable. He is up to something—something sinister; but what it is I cannot make out. . . .

KURT: Alice, your husband is a harmless buffoon—he is forever showing me kindnesses.

ALICE: I know his kindnesses. Be wary of them!

KURT: Now, now. . . .

ALICE: So he has blinded you, too? Don't you sense the danger? Don't you? Don't you notice the snares?

KURT: No.

ALICE: Then you are doomed to come to grief.

KURT: Heaven help us!

ALICE: Imagine my sitting here watching disaster creep upon you like a cat, and pointing it out to you—yet you cannot see it!

KURT: Allan, who is both clearheaded and unprejudiced, sees no danger either. But, then, he has only eyes for Judith; and that, in itself, is an assurance of a happy relationship among us.

ALICE: Do you know Judith—know her well, I mean?

KURT: A flirtatious little vixen with a braid down her back and with skirts that could be a little longer.

ALICE: Precisely. But I saw her the other day dressed up in a

85

long skirt—and then she was a young lady; and when she put up her hair, she did not seem so very young any more.

KURT: I must admit she is rather precocious.

ALICE: And she is playing a game with Allan.

KURT: No harm in that, so long as it is only play.

ALICE: So-o? There is no harm in that, ha!—Edgar will be here any moment now, and he will seat himself in the easy chair there. . . . He is so passionately in love with it that he could steal it.

KURT: He can have it.

ALICE: Let him sit over there, and we'll stay here. And when he says anything—he always talks a lot in the morning—when he talks about trivial things, I'll translate for you. . . .

KURT: Oh, my dear Alice, you are far too clever, far too clever! What should I have to worry about, so long as I look after my quarantine station properly and otherwise conduct myself correctly?

ALICE: You believe in honor and justice, and that sort of thing. . . .

KURT: Yes. Experience has taught me that. There was a time when I believed the opposite; and I paid for it—paid for it dearly.

ALICE: *(With a look of warning.)* He is coming. . . .

KURT: I have never known you to be frightened before.

ALICE: My courage was merely ignorance of the danger.

KURT: Danger? You'll soon have me frightened, too.

ALICE: Oh, how I wish that I could.—Here he comes. . . . *(The Captain enters from the rear. He is in civilian dress, a black redingote, which he wears buttoned; on his head he has an officer's cap, and he carries a silver-topped walking-stick. He greets them with a nod and goes directly to the easy chair and sits down. Alice, to Kurt:)* Let *him* speak first.

THE CAPTAIN: This is a superb chair you have here, my dear Kurt, truly superb.

KURT: It is yours, if you will accept it as a gift.

THE CAPTAIN: It was not my intention to. . . .

KURT: But I meant what I said—sincerely. Think of all you have given me!

THE CAPTAIN: *(Volubly.)* What nonsense! . . . And when I sit here I have a bird's-eye-view of the whole island—of all the walks and thoroughfares—I can see all the people sitting on their verandas—all the ships out on the sea—ships coming and going. . . . You were indeed in luck when you got the best location on this island, which is certainly not an Isle of the Blessed. Or what do you say, Alice? Indeed, it is called 'Little Hell'; and here is where Kurt has built himself a Paradise—but without his Eve, of course . . . for when *she* appeared, Paradise came to an end! I say, do you know that this was once a royal hunting-lodge?

KURT: So I have heard.

THE CAPTAIN: You live royally, Kurt, but I'm ashamed to admit that you have me to thank for that.

ALICE: *(To Kurt.)* Watch out; now he is about to fleece you!

KURT: *(To Edgar.)* I have much to thank you for.

THE CAPTAIN: Don't talk nonsense!—Tell me, did the cases of wine come yet?

KURT: Yes.

THE CAPTAIN: And are you satisfied?

KURT: Very. You can tell your wine dealer I am well pleased.

THE CAPTAIN: His wines are always top quality.

ALICE: *(To Kurt.)* At second rate prices, and you pay the difference.

THE CAPTAIN: What did you say, Alice?

ALICE: I? Nothing.

THE CAPTAIN: Yes—when this quarantine station was in the throes of being established, I seriously thought of applying for the post of quarantine master; and with that in mind I made a study of quarantine methods.

ALICE: *(To Kurt.)* He is lying!

THE CAPTAIN: *(Boastfully.)* I found I could not share the archaic ideas concerning disinfecting methods, which the department heads held. You see, I stood on the side of the

Neptunists—that's the name we gave them because they were in favor of the water method. . . .

KURT: You'll forgive me, but I remember clearly that it was I who preached the water method, and you were for disinfecting by heat, that time.

THE CAPTAIN: I? Nothing of the sort!

ALICE: *(Aloud.)* Yes, I remember that, too.

THE CAPTAIN: You?

KURT: I recall it all the more clearly, since. . . .

THE CAPTAIN: *(Abruptly cutting him off.)* Be that as it may, it doesn't matter! *(His voice growing louder.)* However—we have now arrived at the point when a new set of circumstances. . . . *(To Kurt who is trying to break into his haranguing.)* . . . don't interrupt me . . . when a new set of circumstances has presented itself, and the quarantine service is now in the process of taking a gigantic step forward.

KURT: That reminds me—do you know who it is who has been writing those stupid articles in that periodical?

THE CAPTAIN: *(Turning red in the face.)* I have no idea—but why do you call them stupid?

ALICE: *(To Kurt.)* Watch out! It is he who has written them!

KURT: *(To Alice.)* He? *(To the Captain.)* Well, at any rate, not too judicious, if you so like.

THE CAPTAIN: I don't think you are capable of being the judge of that.

ALICE: Are you going to start a quarrel now?

KURT: Oh no!

THE CAPTAIN: It is not so easy to keep things peaceful on this island, but we ought to set a good example. . . .

KURT: I agree. But can you explain this to me? When I came out here, I at once became friendly with all those in official positions. With the Judge Advocate, in particular, I was on especially intimate terms—as intimate as one can be at our age. Then, after a lapse of time—it was not long after you had recovered from your attack—one after another began showing coldness toward me; and yesterday the Judge Advocate refused to return my greeting when we met on the Promenade. I can't tell you how it hurt my pride. (*The Captain is silent.*) Have you ever encountered any similar behavior toward you?

THE CAPTAIN: No, quite the contrary.

ALICE: (*To Kurt.*) Don't you understand? He has been stealing your friends!

KURT: (*To the Captain.*) I have been wondering whether it could have anything to do with the new stock issue which refused to vote for.

THE CAPTAIN: Oh no!—But just why wouldn't you subscribe to it, tell me?

KURT: Because I had already placed my small savings in your soda water venture. And also because a new issue is an indication that the old stock is shaky.

THE CAPTAIN: (*His mind wandering.*) That's a superb lamp you have there. Where did you get that?

KURT: In the city, of course.

ALICE: (*To Kurt.*) Watch out for your lamp, Kurt!

KURT: (*To the Captain.*) You must not think that I am ungrateful, or that I mistrust you, Edgar. . . .

THE CAPTAIN: Yes, but it doesn't indicate much confidence if you withdraw from a business- undertaking that you have helped to start.

KURT: My dear Edgar, ordinary prudence demands that a person save himself and what is his in time.

THE CAPTAIN: Save, you say? Do you see any danger ahead? Is anybody trying to fleece you?

KURT: Why use such harsh words, Edgar?

THE CAPTAIN: Weren't you satisfied when I helped you to invest your capital at six percent, eh?

KURT: Yes, I even felt grateful.

THE CAPTAIN: You are not grateful—it is not in your nature to be grateful—but that is not your fault.

ALICE: (*To Kurt.*) Listen to him!

KURT: My nature has its shortcomings, no doubt, and my

struggle against them has been far from successful; however, I recognize my obligations. . . .

THE CAPTAIN: Then show it! *(He stretches out his hand and picks up a newspaper on the table.)* Why, what's this? This death notice. . . . *(He reads.)* The senior medical officer of the Ministry of Health is dead!

ALICE: *(To Kurt.)* He is already speculating on how to profit from the corpse!

THE CAPTAIN: *(As if to himself.)* This will bring changes in its wake. . . .

KURT: In which respect?

THE CAPTAIN: *(Gets up.)* We'll see. . . .

ALICE: *(To the Captain.)* Where are you going?

THE CAPTAIN: I must go to the city, I think.

(Suddenly he catches sight of an envelope on the writing-table and picks it up, as if absent-mindedly, reads the sender's address and then lays it on the table.)

Excuse me for being a little absent-minded!

KURT: No harm done.

THE CAPTAIN: Here is Allan's case with his mathematical instruments.—Where is the boy?

KURT: He is out playing with the girls.

THE CAPTAIN: A big boy like him? I don't like that. And I don't want Judith to be running around in that fashion. You must keep an eye on your young gentleman; and I'll take care of my young lady! *(As he walks past the grand piano, he strikes a few notes on it.)* Superb tone this instrument has! A Steinbech? Eh?

KURT: Bechstein.

THE CAPTAIN: Yes, you have done very well, you have! Thanks to me who brought you here.

ALICE: *(To Kurt.)* He is lying—he tried to prevent your appointment.

THE CAPTAIN: Good-bye for a while. . . . I am taking the next boat.

(As he goes out, he gazes covetously at the paintings on the wall.)

ALICE: *(To Kurt with a quizzical look.)* Well?

KURT: Well?

ALICE: I still can't figure out what he is up to. But tell me one thing—the envelope he picked up—from whom was it?

KURT: I am ashamed to admit it—it was my only secret.

ALICE: And he was on the scent of it! You see, as I told you before, he is a sorcerer.—Did the envelope have the sender's address on it?

KURT: It has the name of the Voters' League on it.

ALICE: Then he has guessed your secret. I understand you would like to get the nomination for Parliament. And now you'll see that he gets there instead.

KURT: Has he been thinking of running?

ALICE: No, but he will be from now on. I could read it in his expression while he was examining the envelope.

KURT: Was that the reason he decided to go to the city?

ALICE: No, he decided to do that when he read about the death of the Chief Medical Officer of the Ministry of Health.

KURT: What can he expect to gain from the Medical Officer's death?

ALICE: Well, tell me that! Perhaps he was an enemy of Edgar's, who stood in the way of him and his intrigues?

KURT: If he is really so dreadful as you tell me he is—then one has every reason to be afraid of him.

ALICE: Couldn't you see how greedily he wanted to capture you and tie your hands on the pretext of your owing him a debt of gratitude—a debt which does not exist? He was in no way, for example, instrumental in getting you your post here; on the contrary, he did everything he could to thwart it. He is a man-eater, an insect, a termite, who is bent upon devouring your innards until one day you are hollow as a dead pine. . . . Although he is bound to you by the memory of your childhood friendship, he nonetheless hates you. . . .

KURT: How sharp your wits become when you hate.

ALICE: And dulled when in love. Love both blinds and dulls.

KURT: Oh no, you mustn't say that!

ALICE: Do you know what people mean by a vampire? They

91

say it is the soul of a dead human being in search of a body which it can take possession of as a parasite. Edgar is dead, ever since he collapsed and fell that time. He himself, you see, has no interests of his own, no personality, no initiative. But when he gets hold of someone, he hangs on to him with his tentacles, sends down his suckers, and starts to grow and thrive. Just now *you* are the victim.

KURT: If he comes too near to me, I'll shake him off.

ALICE: Try to shake off a burr, and see how it sticks.—By the way, do you know why he doesn't like to see Judith and Allan together so much?

KURT: I imagine he is afraid they might become emotionally entangled.

ALICE: Nothing of the sort. He wants to marry Judith off—to the Colonel!

KURT: *(Alarmed.)* That old widower!

ALICE: Yes!

KURT: Horrible!—And Judith . . . ?

ALICE: If she could get the General, who is eighty, she would take *him* merely to pique the Colonel, who is sixty. To spite and mortify people—that, you see, is what she lives for. To trample and to bully—that is the watchword of Edgar's family.

KURT: So Judith is like that? That proud, attractive, glorious young girl!

ALICE: Oh yes, I know all that!—May I sit down a moment and write a note?

(Kurt arranges the writing-table for her.)

KURT: Please sit here.

ALICE: *(Removing her gloves, she seats herself.)* Now I shall make an attempt at the art of warfare. My first attempt, when I tried to slay the dragon, was a failure. But since then I have learned how to master the craft.

KURT: You know that you have to load before you can fire, don't you?

ALICE: Oh yes—and this time—with live ammunition! *(Kurt*

92

goes out, left.—Alice sits cogitating, and then writes. Allan rushes in, throws himself face down on the sofa, sobbing in a lace handkerchief. Alice—whom Allan did not notice when he entered—watches him for a moment. Then she gets up, walks over to the sofa, and speaks to him softly.) Allan! *(Allan sits up, embarrassed, and hides the handkerchief behind his back. Alice says tenderly, with true womanly feeling:)* You should not be afraid of me, Allan,—I am not going to harm you. . . . Is anything wrong? Are you ill?

ALLAN: Yes.

ALICE: What is the matter?

ALLAN: I don't know.

ALICE: Have you a headache?

ALLAN: No-o.

ALICE: A pain in the chest? In the heart?

ALLAN: Ye-es.

ALICE: A pain—a pain as if your heart were about to melt away —and then it tugs—and tugs. . . .

ALLAN: How could you know?

ALICE: . . . and you want to die—you wish you were dead—and everything seems so utterly dark and dreary. . . . And you can think of only one—one only, and no one else—but if someone else should also be thinking of that same one—the sorrow falls heavily upon one of them. . . . *(Allan forgets himself and starts plucking at the handkerchief.)* This is a sickness for which there is no cure. You can't eat, can't drink, you do nothing but weep—and oh, how bitterly!—and preferably out in the woods, where no one sees you—for it is the kind of sorrowful affliction everybody laughs at, people being mostly cruel and mean. Ugh! What is it, then, you want of her? Nothing! You dare not kiss her mouth, for then, you think, you would die; and when your thoughts fly to her, you feel a sensation as if death were not far away. And a death it is, my child,—the kind of death that gives life. But at your age you would not understand that. . . . I feel the fragrance of violets—her fragrance. *(She approaches*

93

Allan and gently takes the handkerchief from him.) It is she
—her fragrance—she is everywhere—she is the one and only
one. . . . Oh, my dear boy! *(Allan takes the only way out
and hides his face at Alice's breast.)* You poor boy! You poor
boy! How it must hurt you—how it must hurt! *(She wipes
away his tears with the handkerchief.)* There, there, there!
Cry—cry—then you will feel better! It eases the heart. . . .
But now, Allan, you must be yourself again—be a *m a n*—
else she will not give you a glance—that cruel girl, who does
not mean to be cruel. . . . Has she tormented you? Made
you jealous because of the Lieutenant? Listen to me, my boy!
You must make a friend of the Lieutenant and then you
two can talk about her and compare notes. That usually
eases the pain.

ALLAN: I have no wish to see the Lieutenant!

ALICE: Now, now, my boy! It won't be long before the Lieutenant will be coming to you and want to talk about the
girl and compare notes, because. . . . *(Allan straightens up
with a glint of hope.)* Shall I tell you why? *(Allan gives a
nod of assent.)* Because he is just as unhappy as you are.

ALLAN: *(Beaming.)* You don't mean it?

ALICE: You can be quite certain he is, and whenever Judith
wounds his feelings he needs to unburden himself to someone.—You already seem cheered up. . . .

ALLAN: Doesn't she want the Lieutenant?

ALICE: She wants neither him nor you, my dear Allan—she
wants the Colonel! *(Allan's face shows disappointment and
shock.)* So, it's raining again?—Well, you can't have the handkerchief because Judith is particular about her things and
wants to keep her dozen intact. *(Allan looks foolish.)* Yes,
Allan—that is the way Judith is!—Sit over there now, while
I finish another letter; then I'll let you do an errand for me.
   *(She goes to the writing-table and sits down, continuing
   her writing. The Lieutenant enters from the rear. He
   looks depressed, but without appearing comic. Unconscious of Alice's presence, he makes a straight line to
   Allan.)*

94

THE LIEUTENANT: Cadet Officer. . . . (*Allan rises and stands at attention.*) Sit down, please. (*Alice watches them. The Lieutenant goes up to Allan and seats himself beside him. He sighs, takes out a handkerchief, similar to the one Allan had, and wipes the perspiration off his forehead with it. Allan stares jealously at the handkerchief. The Lieutenant regards Allan with a sad face. Alice coughs. The Lieutenant leaps to his feet, stands rigidly erect, and bows.*)

ALICE: Please sit down.

THE LIEUTENANT: I beg your pardon, Madam . . .

ALICE: No need to apologize. Do sit down and keep Allan company. He feels a little forlorn out here on the island.

> (*She continues writing. The Lieutenant converses embarrassed with Allan in a subdued voice.*)

THE LIEUTENANT: It's frightfully hot.

ALLAN: Oh—yes. . . .

THE LIEUTENANT: Have you finished the Sixth Book yet?

ALLAN: I am in the midst of the last proposition.

THE LIEUTENANT: A little tricky, isn't it? (*Silence.*) Have you—have you been playing any tennis today?

ALLAN: N-no, the sun was too hot.

THE LIEUTENANT: (*In agony, yet without being comical.*) Yes, it is frightfully hot today.

ALLAN: (*In a whisper.*) Yes, it is very hot.
> (*Silence.*)

THE LIEUTENANT: Have you—have you been out sailing today?

ALLAN: No-o. I couldn't get anyone to take care of the fore-sail.

THE LIEUTENANT: Would you care to entrust me with it?

ALLAN: That would be asking too much of you, Lieutenant.

THE LIEUTENANT: Not at all, not at all!—Do you think that—that we will have a good breeze today—say, about midday? That's the only time I am free.

ALLAN: At noon the wind usually dies down, and—and Miss Judith has her lesson then.

THE LIEUTENANT: (*Downcast.*) Oh! Oh, well. . . . H'm.—Do you think that. . . .

ALICE: Would one of you gentlemen care to deliver a letter

for me? (*The two young men look at each other suspiciously.*) It's for Miss Judith. (*Allan and the Lieutenant leap to their feet and rush over to Alice. They do this with a certain dignity, however, with an effort to conceal their excitement.*) I see we have two lettercarriers. So much the better—then the letter will certainly be in safe hands. (*She hands the letter to the Lieutenant.*) Oh, Lieutenant, may I have that handkerchief? It has to go into the wash. My daughter is rather particular about her finery, and besides is a little parsimonious. Give it to me, please.—I don't wish to laugh at you, but you must not make fools of yourselves—unnecessarily. And I don't think the Colonel wants to be an Othello! (*She takes the handkerchief from him.*) Be on your way now, young men, and try to hide your feelings as best you can. (*The Lieutenant bows and goes out, with Allan following him. Alice calls after him:*) Allan!

ALLAN: (*Reluctantly stopping in the doorway.*) Yes, Aunt Alice.

ALICE: Stay here, if you don't want to be more hurt than you can stand.

ALLAN: Yes, but *h e* is going to her!

ALICE: Then let him get burned. But you take care!

ALLAN: I don't want to!

ALICE: You'll end by shedding tears. And then I'll have the trouble of consoling you.

ALLAN: I want to go along with him!

ALICE: Then go! But come back here, you harebrained young scamp, so that I may have a good laugh at you!

    (*Allan races after the Lieutenant. Alice sits down at the writing-table again and continues her writing.*)

KURT: (*Enters.*) Alice, I have received an anonymous letter, which disturbs me.

ALICE: Have you noticed that Edgar has become a totally different person since he discarded his uniform? I never thought a uniform could make so much difference in a person.

KURT: You did not answer my question.

ALICE: That was not a question. It was a piece of intelligence. What are you worried about?

KURT: Everything.

ALICE: He went to the city. Whenever he goes to the city, it means that something sinister is afoot.

KURT: But how can I possibly do anything to thwart it when I haven't the faintest idea from where the attack is coming?

ALICE: *(Putting the letter in an envelope and sealing it.)* Now we'll see if I have guessed correctly. . . .

KURT: Are you willing to help me, then?

ALICE: Yes—but only so far as my own interests allow it. Mine —meaning my children's.

KURT: I quite understand.—Do you hear, Alice, how silent it is outside—on the sea—on the island—everywhere?

ALICE: But from beyond the stillness I hear voices—murmuring —outcries—shrieking—screaming. . . .

KURT: Hush! I hear it, too. . . . No, it was only the sea gulls. . . .

ALICE: I hear something else. . . . And now I am going to the post office—with this!

    (She gestures with the letter.)

END OF SCENE 1

ACT I   SCENE 2

The same setting.

Allan is sitting at the writing-table, studying.

Judith stands in the doorway. She is wearing a tennis hat and is carrying the handle-bar of a bicycle.

JUDITH: May I borrow your screw-wrench?

ALLAN: *(Without looking up.)* No, you may not.

JUDITH: You are rude to me because you think I am running after you.

ALLAN: *(Without being snappish.)* I am neither rude nor anything else, but I should like to be left alone.

JUDITH: *(Coming closer to him.)* Allan. . . .

ALLAN: Well, what do you want?

JUDITH: You must not be angry with me.

ALLAN: I am not angry.

JUDITH: Will you give me your hand on that?

ALLAN: *(Tractably.)* I don't want to shake hands with you—but I am not angry. What is it you want of me, anyhow?

JUDITH: You are so silly. . . .

ALLAN: You are welcome to think so.

JUDITH: You think I am mean and cruel and nothing else, don't you?

ALLAN: No, I don't—for I know that, when you want to be, you can be both friendly and nice.

JUDITH: Well, I can't help it if you—if you and the lieutenant go around shedding tears in the woods. Why do you weep? *(Allan, embarrassed, does not reply.)* Tell me. . . . You never see *me* cry. And why is it that you have become such good friends of late? What do you talk about when you saunter about, arm in arm. *(Allan is speechless.)* Allan—you will soon learn to appreciate what I am, and you will find out that if

98

I care for anyone, I can be of help to him. And—even though I don't like to tattle, I can give you a piece of information. . . . You must be prepared for. . . .

ALLAN: Prepared for what?

JUDITH: Some unpleasantness.

ALLAN: From whom?

JUDITH: From where you least expect it.

ALLAN: I am quite accustomed to annoyances and have not had too much fun out of life. . . . What is it that's in store for me now?

JUDITH: *(Pensively.)* You poor boy!—Give me your hand! *(Allan gives her his hand.)* Look at me!—are you afraid to look at me?

(Allan rushes out, right, in order to conceal his emotion.)

THE LIEUTENANT: *(Enters from the rear.)* I beg your pardon—I thought the Cadet Officer was. . . .

JUDITH: Lieutenant! I'd like you to be my friend and let me confide something to you. . . .

THE LIEUTENANT: It makes me happy to think that you trust me!

JUDITH: I do.—Let me ask you in just a few words—not to desert Allan if anything unfortunate should happen!

THE LIEUTENANT: Unfortunate . . . ?

JUDITH: You will hear about it shortly—even today perhaps. . . . Do you like Allan?

THE LIEUTENANT: That young man is my best student, and I respect him as well. He has stability of character. And that is something we need all too often . . . *(With emphasis.)* . . . strength to bear up under adversities; in a word, to endure, to suffer.

JUDITH: That was more than one word, I'd say. However, you do like Allan, don't you?

THE LIEUTENANT: Yes, I do.

JUDITH: Then go and find him and keep him company.

THE LIEUTENANT: That was why I came here—for that purpose only.

JUDITH: I had not supposed otherwise—as you seem to imply.—
Allan went out that way.

(She indicates the door on the right.)

THE LIEUTENANT: *(Goes reluctantly toward the right.)* Yes—I'll
keep him company.

JUDITH: Do that, please.

(The Lieutenant goes out.)

ALICE: *(Enters from the rear.)* What are you doing here?

JUDITH: I came to borrow a bicycle wrench.

ALICE: Will you listen to me for a moment?

JUDITH: Certainly, I will. *(Alice seats herself on the sofa; Judith
remains standing.)* But tell me quickly what you have to say.
I can't stand long lectures.

ALICE: Lectures?—Well, then, put your hair up and change into
a long dress.

JUDITH: Why?

ALICE: Because you are no longer a child. And you are too
young to go flirting about, acting younger than your age.

JUDITH: What are you leading up to?

ALICE: That you are old enough to marry. And that your way
of dressing is causing offense to people.

JUDITH: Then I'll conform to your wishes.

ALICE: You have understood, then?

JUDITH: Yes, indeed.

ALICE: On all points?

JUDITH: Even the most delicate!

ALICE: Will you at the same time discontinue playing a game
—with Allan?

JUDITH: You like me to be in earnest, then?

ALICE: Yes.

JUDITH: Then we may as well begin immediately.

*(She puts away the handle-bar, lets down her bicycle
skirt, and arranges her braid in a knot, which she fastens
on top of her head with a hairpin, that she takes from
her mother's hair.)*

ALICE: One does not do one's toilet at the home of strangers.

100

JUDITH: How do I look now?—I am quite prepared now! And so—come who may!

ALICE: Now you look respectable at least.—And from now on you leave Allan in peace.

JUDITH: I don't understand what is in your mind?

ALICE: Don't you see how unhappy he is?

JUDITH: Yes, I think I have noticed it, but I can't understand why.

ALICE: That is where your strength lies. But just wait—and some day you, too, will suffer! Oh, yes!—Now go home, and don't forget—that you are now dressed in a long skirt!

JUDITH: Am I to walk differently now?

ALICE: Go ahead—try!

JUDITH: *(Tries to walk like a lady.)* Oh, my feet are tied—I am tied—I can't run any more!

ALICE: Yes, my child, now the procession begins—the slow march toward the unknown, which one knows all about beforehand, yet must pretend not to know. Shorter steps—and slower, much slower, much slower. You must get rid of the shoes you've been wearing as a child and now wear young ladies' shoes, Judith.—You don't remember when you discarded your baby socks and stepped into shoes, do you, Judith?

JUDITH: This is more than I can stand!

ALICE: Still you must—you must!
(Judith goes over to Alice and kisses her casually on the check. Then she walks with dignity, like a lady, toward the door, rear, leaving the handle-bar behind.)

JUDITH: Good-bye.

KURT: *(Enters from the left.)* You are here already?

ALICE: Yes.

KURT: Has Edgar come back yet?

ALICE: Yes.

KURT: How was he dressed?

ALICE: In gala uniform. Consequently he has been to see the Colonel. He wore two decorations.

KURT: Two? I knew he would be given the Order of the Sword on his retirement. What could the other one be?

ALICE: I am not familiar with these things, but it has a white cross on a red field.

KURT: Ah! Then it was a Portuguese order.—Let me think! The articles he wrote in that periodical—didn't they give an account of the quarantine stations in Portuguese harbors?

ALICE: Yes, I seem to remember they did.

KURT: And he has never been in Portugal, has he?

ALICE: Never.

KURT: But I have.

ALICE: Why should you always be so communicative? He is such a good listener, and he has such an excellent memory.

KURT: You don't think that Judith—is in any way responsible for his getting this decoration, do you?

ALICE: Oh now, Kurt! There is a limit . . . *(She gets up.)* . . . and you are overstepping it. . . .

KURT: Are we going to start quarreling now?

ALICE: That is up to you. But do not meddle in my interests!

KURT: If they run counter to mine, I must deal with them, even if only lightly.—Here he comes now.

ALICE: This is the time for action.

KURT: What are you going to do?

ALICE: We shall see.

KURT: Let us proceed to the attack then, for this state of siege is tearing at my nerves. I haven't a friend left on the whole island.

ALICE: Let's see now!—He'll be taking the easy chair, no doubt, so you sit on this side, then I can prompt you.

(The Captain enters from the rear. He is in dress uniform and wears the Order of the Sword and the Portuguese Order of Christ.)

THE CAPTAIN: Good morning. So this is where we meet!

ALICE: You are tired. Sit down. *(The Captain, contrary to expectations, seats himself on the sofa, to the right.)* Make yourself comfortable.

THE CAPTAIN: I am comfortable here.—You are much too considerate.

ALICE: *(To Kurt.)* Be careful—he is suspicious of us.

THE CAPTAIN: *(Irritably.)* What was that you said?

ALICE: *(To Kurt.)* I think he has been drinking.

THE CAPTAIN: *(Boorishly and savagely.)* No, he has not. *(Silence.)* Well—what have you been doing to amuse yourselves?

ALICE: And you?

THE CAPTAIN: Are you looking at my decorations?

ALICE: No.

THE CAPTAIN: No, I can well imagine—you are jealous. Otherwise it is customary to congratulate a person when he has had a decoration conferred on him.

ALICE: *(Exaggeratedly; sarcastically.)* We congratulate you.

THE CAPTAIN: Instead of laurel wreaths given to actresses, *we* are given honors like these.

ALICE: *(To Kurt.)* Now he is dragging down the wreaths that hang on the wall in the tower. . . .

THE CAPTAIN: Which your brothers gave you.

ALICE: Oh, keep quiet!

THE CAPTAIN: And which I have had to salaam to for twenty-five years . . . and which it has taken me twenty-five years to expose.

ALICE: Have you been seeing my brother?

THE CAPTAIN: A good deal. *(Alice is crushed.)* How about you, Kurt? You are not saying anything.

KURT: I am waiting.

THE CAPTAIN: Oh, say! I suppose you have heard the great news?

KURT: No.

THE CAPTAIN: It's not precisely pleasant for me to be the one to bring . . .

KURT: Go ahead—don't hesitate.

THE CAPTAIN: The soda factory has crashed.

KURT: That is most unfortunate.—How will that affect you?

THE CAPTAIN: I'm in luck—I sold out in time.

103

KURT: That was sensible of you.

THE CAPTAIN: But how about you?

KURT: Wiped out!

THE CAPTAIN: You have only yourself to blame. You should have sold out in time, or taken the new stock.

KURT: If I had, I'd have lost that, too.

THE CAPTAIN: Nothing of the kind. For then the company would have survived.

KURT: Not the company, but the board members; and I considered the new stock issue exclusively a collection for them.

THE CAPTAIN: And can this way of looking at the matter save you now, do you think?

KURT: No—I'll be losing everything I have.

THE CAPTAIN: Everything?

KURT: Everything—down to the last stick of furniture!

THE CAPTAIN: This is dreadful!

KURT: I've been through worse.

(Silence.)

THE CAPTAIN: That's what happens when amateurs try to speculate.

KURT: You astonish me, for you know that if I had not subscribed, I would have been boycotted. . . . "As a subsidiary means of livelihood of the coastal population, of the toilers of the sea. . . . unlimited capital, as inexhaustible as the sea itself. . . . philanthropy and national prosperity," and so forth. That is what you had printed and advertised—and now you speak of it as speculation!

THE CAPTAIN: *(Unaffected.)* What do you intend to do now?

KURT: Put my property up at auction, I expect.

THE CAPTAIN: You'll be doing the wise thing.

KURT: What do you mean by that?

THE CAPTAIN: Just what I said. There are, namely,— *(Slowly, with emphasis.)* certain changes to be made here. . . .

KURT: Here—on the island . . . ?

THE CAPTAIN: Yes. Your official residence, for example, will be moved to more modest quarters.

KURT: H'm.

THE CAPTAIN: You see, the plan is to place the quarantine station on the outer shore of the island, by the open sea.

KURT: My original idea!

THE CAPTAIN: *(Drily.)* I don't know anything about that—I am not familiar with your ideas in the matter. However—this provides you with a suitable excuse to get rid of your furniture now, so that the scandal won't be too apparent. . . .

KURT: What did you say?

THE CAPTAIN: The scandal! *(Working himself up into a temper.)* For it is a scandal to come to a new post and immediately get involved in a financial mess which cannot bring anything but unpleasantness to, and reflect upon, the relatives—especially the relatives.

KURT: I should think I am the one who will suffer most!

THE CAPTAIN: I want to tell you one thing, Kurt: if you hadn't had me to intervene for you, you would have been discharged from your post.

KURT: That, too!

THE CAPTAIN: You have a tendency to be a little careless. Complaints have been made about your performance of your duties.

KURT: You don't mean justified complaints?

THE CAPTAIN: Cha!—for in spite of your otherwise respectable qualities, you *are* careless! Don't interrupt me—you are *exceedingly careless!*

KURT: This is really astonishing!

THE CAPTAIN: However—the change I just mentioned is planned to take place in the immediate future. For that reason I should advise you to have the auction without delay, or try to dispose of your property and household effects privately.

KURT: Privately? Where can I find a buyer here?

THE CAPTAIN: You couldn't expect me to make myself at home in your furniture, could you? That would be something to talk about. . . . *(By fits and starts.)*—h'm—especially—if one—if one considers—what happened—once in the past. . . .

105

KURT: What did happen? Or, do you mean—what did *not* happen?

THE CAPTAIN: *(Abruptly changing the subject.)* Alice is so quiet! What ails you, old girl? You are not sad, are you?

ALICE: I am thinking. . . .

THE CAPTAIN: Oh, heavens! Are you thinking? But you have to think fast, clearly, and correctly, if it is to do you any good!—So, go ahead and think! One—two—three!—Haha! You can't! Well, then, let me try!—Where is Judith?

ALICE: She is somewhere about.

THE CAPTAIN: Where is Allan? *(Alice does not answer.)* Where is the Lieutenant? *(Alice remains silent.)* Tell me, Kurt, what are your plans for Allan now?

KURT: Plans?

THE CAPTAIN: Yes, you can't afford to let him stay in the artillery any longer.

KURT: Perhaps not.

THE CAPTAIN: You have to try to get him into a cheap infantry regiment—up in Norrland, or somewhere far up in the north.

KURT: In Norrland?

THE CAPTAIN: Yes—or you may prefer to have him change to a more practical vocation, why not?—If I were you, I would have him take a position in an office. I don't see why not. . . . *(Kurt is silent.)* . . . in these enlightened times! Cha!—Alice is so exceptionally silent today. Yes, my children, such are the ups and downs on the see-saw of life. . . . One moment you are up in the air, looking down and around you with cockiness; the next you are all the way down—and then you are up again! And so on, and so forth. . . . That was that, yes. . . . *(To Alice.)* Did you say anything? *(Alice shakes her head.)* We can expect visitors here in a few days. . . .

ALICE: Are you speaking to me?

THE CAPTAIN: We can expect visitors in a few days. Important visitors.

ALICE: Who?

THE CAPTAIN: You see! You are interested!—Now you can sit

106

there and guess who it is, and while you are guessing you might take another look at this letter and read it again!

(He hands her an opened letter.)

ALICE: My letter! Opened! Returned by the postmaster!

THE CAPTAIN: *(Getting up.)* Yes, in my capacity as head of the family and your guardian, I must exercise vigilance over the most sacred interests of the family; and any attempt to sever the family ties through correspondence of a criminal nature shall be cut off with an iron hand. Cha! *(Alice is overcome.)* I am not dead, remember that, but you must not get angry now when I am about to lift us all out of undeserved humiliation—undeserved *on my part,* at least!

ALICE: Judith! Judith!

THE CAPTAIN: And Holofernes—I suppose? Bah!

(He goes out, rear.)

KURT: Who is this man?

ALICE: I don't know.

KURT: We are beaten!

ALICE: Yes—we are beaten!

KURT: He has gnawed me out completely, and with such infernal cleverness that I can't accuse him of anything.

ALICE: *(Ironically.)* Accuse him? No, on the contrary, you owe him a debt of gratitude.

KURT: Is he conscious of what he is doing, I wonder?

ALICE: I can't believe he is. He does what his nature impels him to do and follows his instincts. For the moment he seems to be smiled upon by the powers that mete out fortune and misfortune, good and evil.

KURT: I imagine it is the Colonel who is coming here?

ALICE: Probably. And that is why Allan must be got rid of.

KURT: And you find that justified?

ALICE: Yes, I do.

KURT: Then we shall go our separate ways.

ALICE: *(Preparing to leave.)* But not too far apart. . . . We shall undoubtedly meet again.

KURT: No doubt.

ALICE: And do you know where?

KURT: Here.

ALICE: You have that feeling.

KURT: It is easy to guess: he takes my house and buys the household effects.

ALICE: I think you are right.—But do not desert me!

KURT: Not for so trifling a thing as that.

ALICE: Good-bye.

    (She goes out.)

KURT: Good-bye.

END OF SCENE 2

ACT II

The setting is the same.

It is a cloudy, rainy day.

Alice and Kurt enter from the rear, both in raincoats and carrying umbrellas.

ALICE: So you finally set foot here!—Kurt, I cannot be so cruel as to bid you welcome—in your own home.

KURT: Oh, why not? I have been through three compulsory sales, and even worse, so you couldn't offend me.

ALICE: Did *he* summon you here?

KURT: He sent me a formal summons—but what the reason for it is I am at a loss to know.

ALICE: But he is not your superior?

KURT: No, but he has made himself king of this island. And if anyone dares to oppose him, he immediately resorts to the use of the Colonel's name, and then they all submit.—Tell me, is it today the Colonel is due here?

ALICE: He is expected—but I can't be certain about it.—Please sit down.

KURT: *(Seating himself.)* Everything looks the same here.

ALICE: Don't let your mind dwell on it! Don't open up the wound and be in pain again!

KURT: Pain? I find this merely a little strange—as strange as the man himself.—Do you know that when I first made his acquaintance as a boy, I kept away from him. But he pursued me, flattered me, offered to be of help, and caught me in his net; and though I tried to escape, it was in vain. Now I am his slave!

ALICE: And why? It is *he*, who owes *you* a debt—and yet you are made to pay for it.

109

KURT: After having ruined me, he has offered to help Allan through his examination.

ALICE: And for that you will have to pay dearly.—Are you still a candidate for the Parliament?

KURT: Yes, as far as I can see nothing stands in the way of it. *(Silence.)*

ALICE: Is Allan really leaving today?

KURT: Yes—unless I can prevent it.

ALICE: It was a short-lived happiness for you both.

KURT: That, like everything else except life itself, which is dreadfully long.

ALICE: It is, indeed.—Won't you come into the drawing-room and wait there instead? To me the atmosphere in this room is stifling—even if it does not trouble you.

KURT: Just as you wish.

ALICE: I feel ashamed—ashamed beyond words—but there is nothing I can do to change things.

KURT: Let us go in there, then, if you like.

ALICE: Yes, and besides—someone is coming.

(They go out, right.—The Captain and Allan enter from the rear. Both are in uniform, with cloaks.)

THE CAPTAIN: Sit down here, my boy. I want to have a talk with you. *(Seats himself in the easy chair. Allan sits down on the chair on the right.)* If it were not raining today, I could sit here and enjoy looking at the sea. *(Silence.)* Well, then—so you don't wish to leave?

ALLAN: I don't like to leave my father.

THE CAPTAIN: Your father, yes—he is a most unfortunate man. *(Silence.)* And parents rarely understand what is best for their children. There are, of course, exceptions, I'll admit. H'm. . . . Tell me, Allan, do you keep in touch with your mother?

ALLAN: Yes, I get a letter from her now and then.

THE CAPTAIN: You know that she is your guardian, don't you?

ALLAN: Ye-es.

THE CAPTAIN: And you know, Allan, that your mother has

110

given me power-of-attorney to act on her behalf.

ALLAN: No, I didn't know that.

THE CAPTAIN: Now you know, however. Consequently, all discussion pertaining to your career is terminated, and you are going to Norrland.

ALLAN: But I have no means to. . . .

THE CAPTAIN: All that has been taken care of.

ALLAN: In that case, all I can do is to thank you, Uncle.

THE CAPTAIN: You, at least, are grateful—something I can't say about everybody. H'm. *(Raising his voice.)* The Colonel. . . . Do you know the Colonel?

ALLAN: *(Nonplussed.)* No, I don't.

THE CAPTAIN: The Col-onel . . . *(Holding on the word.)* . . . is a particular friend of mine . . . *(In a more casual manner.)* . . . as you undoubtedly know. H'm. The Colonel has condescended to take an interest in my family, including my wife's relations. Through his intercession, the Colonel has procured the necessary means for you to complete your training course.—So now you know to whom you are indebted— and to whom your father is indebted: the Colonel!—Have I made this sufficiently clear to you? *(Allan bows deferentially.)* Now go and pack your belongings! The money will be given to you at the gangway as you go ashore. And now—good-bye, my boy. *(He extends a finger to Allan as a good-bye gesture.)* Good-bye.

> *(He gets up and goes out, left.—Allan, now alone, stands dejected; he looks around the room. Judith enters from the rear. Dressed exquisitely, in a long skirt and with her hair done up, she carries an umbrella. Over her dress she wears a hooded raincoat or cape.)*

JUDITH: Is that you, Allan?

ALLAN: *(Turns about and scrutinizes carefully her appearance.)* Is this really you, Judith?

JUDITH: You don't recognize me? But where have you been all this time? . . . What are you looking at? . . . My long dress— and my hair. . . . You haven't seen me like this before?

ALLAN: No-o. . . .

JUDITH: Do I look like somebody's wife, eh? *(Allan turns away from her. Judith, in a more serious tone.)* What are you doing here?

ALLAN: I came to say good-bye.

JUDITH: What's that? Are you—are you going away?

ALLAN: I am being transferred to Norrland.

JUDITH: *(Struck dumb.)* To Norrland?—When are you leaving?

ALLAN: Today.

JUDITH: Whose idea is this?

ALLAN: Your father's.

JUDITH: I might have guessed. *(She walks up and down, stamping her foot.)* I wish you could stay here today.

ALLAN: And meet the Colonel?

JUDITH: What do you know about the Colonel? Is it definite that you are leaving?

ALLAN: I have no choice in the matter. And besides—now I *want* to go.

(Silence.)

JUDITH: Why do you want to?

ALLAN: I want to get away from here. Out into the world.

JUDITH: Yes, I know how you feel, Allan. It is too confined here, it is unbearable—with all their speculating—in soda water and in human beings. *(Silence. With true emotion and feeling.)* Allan—I am sure you have learned that it is not in my nature to feel so deeply that I suffer pain. . . . but now—now I am beginning to realize that I *can* suffer. . . .

ALLAN: You—Judith!

JUDITH: Yes—now I am beginning to feel it . . . ! *(She presses both hands to her breast.)* Oh—I suffer so terribly! Oh!

ALLAN: Where does it hurt?

JUDITH: I don't know. . . . I am suffocating. . . . I think I'm dying!

ALLAN: Judith!

JUDITH: *(Gives a loud cry.)* Oh!—Is this how you poor boys feel?

ALLAN: If I were as hardhearted as you, I would laugh!

112

JUDITH: I am not hardhearted! I just didn't know any better. I won't let you go! . . .

ALLAN: I must.

JUDITH: Then go—but give me something to remember you by.

ALLAN: What have I that I can give you?

JUDITH: *(From the depth of her bruised heart.)* Allan! Oh—this is more than I can bear. . . . *(With her hands pressed against her heart, she shrieks hysterically.)* Oh, the pain, the pain! What have you done to me? I don't want to live any longer after this! Allan—don't go—not alone! Let us go together—let us take the small sloop—the small white sloop—and let us sail away, but with sails flattened in—there is a good breeze blowing—and we shall sail until we go down to the depths of the sea—out to sea—away out into the beyond, where there is no eelgrass to snare us and no nettle-fish to sting. What do you say, Allan? Say something!—But we should have washed the sails yesterday—they should be snowy white—for at that final moment I wish to see everything in pure white—and then you shall swim with me clinging to your arm, until you have no strength left—and then we shall sink—together. . . . *(With a sudden change.)* Wouldn't that be a beautiful way to end it all—much better than going about grieving and sending clandestine letters which Father will open, and then sneer and rail at. Allan! *(She takes hold of his arm and shakes him.)* Listen to me!

ALLAN: *(Regarding her with radiant eyes.)* Judith! Judith! Why haven't you spoken like this before?

JUDITH: Because I didn't know! How could I have told you what I had not felt?

ALLAN: And now I must leave you. . . . But perhaps it is for the best—the only thing I can do. . . . I can't compete with someone as . . . someone who—who . . .

JUDITH: Don't speak of the Colonel!

ALLAN: Isn't it true that. . . .

JUDITH: It is—and it isn't. . . .

ALLAN: Can't you make it *untrue*—put an end to it?

113

JUDITH: Yes—now I shall—within an hour.

ALLAN: And you will keep your word? I can wait—I can be patient—I can work. . . . Oh, Judith!

JUDITH: Don't go yet.—How long must I wait?

ALLAN: One year!

JUDITH: *(Ecstatically.)* One year? I shall wait a thousand years, and if you should not come to me then, I shall turn the heavens about so that the sun will be rising in the West. . . . Hush—someone is coming. . . . We must part now, Allan! Don't speak a word! Take me into your arms! *(They embrace.)* But you must not kiss me. . . . *(She turns her head away).* Now go—go now!

> *(Allan goes to the rear and puts on his cloak. Then they spontaneously rush into each other's arms, and Judith is hidden inside Allan's cloak. They momentarily kiss. Allan runs out. Judith throws herself, face down, on the sofa and sobs. In the next moment Allan returns, rushes over to Judith and kneels beside her.)*

ALLAN: No, I cannot go! I cannot leave you!

JUDITH: *(Rising.)* If you only knew how beautiful you are this moment! If you could only see yourself!

ALLAN: Nonsense, no man is ever beautiful. But you, Judith—you. . . . Oh, when you acted so tenderly just now—then I discovered in you another Judith—and *that* Judith is mine. . . . But if you should break faith with me now—then I shall die. . . .

JUDITH: I feel as if I could die! Oh, if I could only die now, this very moment, while I am happy!

ALLAN: Somebody is coming. . . .

JUDITH: Let them come! I have no fear of anything—not of anything in the whole wide world—any longer! Oh, I wish you would take me with you inside your cloak . . . *(She playfully hides beneath his cloak.)* . . . and that I could fly with you to Norrland! What shall we do up there in Norrland? Become riflemen—one of those with plumes in their hats? They look so chic, and they would be so becoming to you. *(She*

*fusses with his hair, and he kisses the tips of her fingers, one
by one, after which he presses a kiss on her boot.)* What are
you doing, silly boy! You'll get shoe blacking on your lips!
(Getting up abruptly, in mock anger.) Now I can't kiss you
any more!—Let us go! I am coming with you!

ALLAN: No—they would arrest me then!

JUDITH: Then I want to be arrested with you!

ALLAN: They wouldn't do that. . . . Now we *must* part!

JUDITH: Then I'll swim after the steamer . . . and you'll have
to jump overboard and save me—and then it'll be printed
in the newspapers—and then we'll be engaged! Shall we do
that? Shall we?

ALLAN: You can still jest!

JUDITH: There will be time enough for tears!—Say good-bye to
me now. . . .

> *(They fly into each other's arms, and then Allan, fol-
> lowed by Judith, walks slowly out through the door in
> the rear, which is left open. They can be seen embracing
> in the rain, outside.)*

ALLAN: You'll be getting wet, Judith.

JUDITH: I don't care!

> *(They tear away from each other. Allan leaves. Judith
> remains standing in the rain and wind, which tugs at
> her hair and clothes as she stands waving her handker-
> chief. Then Judith rushes inside, throws herself on the
> sofa, covering her face with her hands.)*

ALICE: *(Enters and sees Judith. She goes to her.)* What's this I
see? Are you sick?—Stand up and let me look at you! *(Judith
gets up. Alice regards her intently.)* You are not sick. . . . So
I am not going to comfort you.

> *(She goes out, left.)*

> *(Judith returns to her position on the sofa. The Lieu-
> tenant enters from the rear. Judith gets up and puts on
> her raincoat and hood.)*

JUDITH: Will you do me a favor and come with me to the telegraph office, Lieutenant?

THE LIEUTENANT: Yes, if I can be of service to you, Miss Judith, —but I don't know whether it would be entirely proper. . . .

JUDITH: So much the better. That is exactly why I want you to come—so that you can compromise me—but without any illusions on your part. . . . You go ahead!

(They go out, rear. The Captain and Alice enter from the left. The Captain is dressed in fatigue uniform. He seats himself in the easy chair.)

THE CAPTAIN: Have him come in.

(Alice goes to the right and opens the door. Then she seats herself on the sofa. Kurt enters from the right.)

KURT: You wish to see me?

THE CAPTAIN: *(In a pleasant yet somewhat condescending tone.)* Yes, I have a number of things of importance to tell you. —Sit down!

KURT: *(Seating himself on the chair to the right.)* I am all ears.

THE CAPTAIN: Well, then. . . . *(Spouting.)* You are aware that our quarantine service has been sadly neglected for very nearly a century now . . . h'm. . . .

ALICE: *(To Kurt.)* The candidate for the Parliament speaking now. . . .

THE CAPTAIN: But in view of the unprecedented advances in every. . . .

ALICE: He is going to talk about communications, of course.

THE CAPTAIN: . . . in every possible direction, the government has been contemplating making provisions for expanding the scope of its service. In order to carry out this plan, the Ministry of Health has appointed inspectors—and. . . .

ALICE: *(To Kurt.)* He is talking like a phonograph record.

THE CAPTAIN: . . . and—I may as well tell you now as later—I have been appointed an inspector of Quarantine.

(There is a silence.)

KURT: My congratulations!—and at the same time I pay you my respects.

THE CAPTAIN: Because of the family ties that exist between us, there will be no change in our personal relationship. There is, however, a certain other matter, of which I would like to speak. Your son Allan has—at my request—been transferred to an infantry regiment in Norrland.

KURT: But I object to that.

THE CAPTAIN: Your wishes in this matter are subordinate to what his mother wants. And as his mother has authorized me to act on her behalf, I have made the decision I just mentioned.

KURT: (*Sarcastically.*) I admire you!

THE CAPTAIN: Is that how you are affected at a moment like this—when you are to be separated from your son? Haven't you any feelings—any human feelings?

KURT: You mean you would like to see me suffer?

THE CAPTAIN: Yes.

KURT: It would give you joy to see me suffer.

THE CAPTAIN: Can you really suffer, can you?—Once I was taken ill—you were present at the time—and all I can remember was an expression on your face—an expression of undisguised elation.

ALICE: That is a lie. Kurt sat beside your bed all that night and helped to calm you when your pangs of conscience became too much for you to bear. And when you recovered, you forgot to be grateful. . . .

THE CAPTAIN: (*Pretending not to have heard Alice.*) Consequently Allan must leave.

KURT: Who is going to pay for it?

THE CAPTAIN: I have taken care of that, that is, we—a—a group of us, who have taken an interest in the young man and his future.

KURT: A group of. . . .

THE CAPTAIN: Yes.—And just so that you may see that everything has been done correctly, I'll let you take a look at these lists.

(*He hands Kurt some sheets of paper.*)

KURT: Lists? (*He reads.*) Why, these are nothing but pleas for charity!

THE CAPTAIN: Call it what you like.

KURT: Have you been begging for my son?

THE CAPTAIN: Are you ungrateful again? An ungrateful person is the heaviest burden upon this earth.

KURT: Now I am dead socially. And my candidacy is done for!

THE CAPTAIN: What candidacy?

KURT: For Parliament, of course!

THE CAPTAIN: You really did not dream you would get nominated, did you? Especially since I, as you might have known —I being the senior resident here—intend to run for that office. This indicates that you underrate me!

KURT: Well—so now that, too, is finished.

THE CAPTAIN: It doesn't seem to disturb you very much.

KURT: Now you have taken everything. Is there anything else you want?

THE CAPTAIN: *Have* you anything else? And have you anything to reproach me with? Think hard if there is anything you can reproach me for!

(Silence.)

KURT: Strictly speaking, there isn't anything. Everything has been done correctly and lawfully, as between honest, respectable citizens in everyday life!

THE CAPTAIN: You say this with a resignation which I should like to call cynical. But your whole nature has a predisposition to cynicism, my dear Kurt, and there are times when I am tempted to share Alice's opinion of you that you are a hypocrite—a hypocrite of the very first order!

KURT: *(Calmly.)* Is that what Alice thinks?

ALICE: *(To Kurt.)* I did think so at one time, but don't any more. To be able to bear what you have had to bear takes immeasurable courage, or—it might take something else!

THE CAPTAIN: I think we may now consider the discussion closed. Suppose you go and say good-bye to Allan, Kurt, since he is leaving by the next boat.

KURT: So soon?—Ah well, I've been through worse.

THE CAPTAIN: You say that so often that I am beginning to wonder what you could have done in America.

KURT: What I could have done? I'll tell you. I was beset by misfortune, that's all. And every human being has the undeniable right to be subjected to misfortune.

THE CAPTAIN: *(Cuttingly.)* There are misfortunes brought on by your own doings. . . . Were yours that kind?

KURT: Isn't that a question of conscience?

THE CAPTAIN: *(Rudely.)* Have you a conscience? You?

KURT: There are wolves, and there are sheep. To be a sheep is not considered any great human asset; but I would rather be a sheep than a wolf.

THE CAPTAIN: Haven't you heard the old saying that everyone forges his own destiny, eh?

KURT: And does that always hold true?

THE CAPTAIN: Haven't you learned that a man's own strength. . . .

KURT: Yes, I do know that—ever since the night when your own strength failed you and you lay prostrate on the floor.

THE CAPTAIN: *(Raising his voice.)* A man of my merits—yes, you may look at me—who has been pitted against the world for fifty years—and who has finally come out on top—through perseverance, by being loyal and true to duty—through energy and—*and* honesty!

ALICE: You should leave that to others to say.

THE CAPTAIN: That's something they don't do, for they are jealous. However—we have visitors coming. . . . My daughter, Judith, is to meet her intended here today. . . . Where is Judith?

ALICE: She is out.

THE CAPTAIN: In this rain?—Send for her.

KURT: Do you mind if I leave now?

THE CAPTAIN: No, stay—you stay!—Is Judith dressed? Dressed properly?

ALICE: Yes, sufficiently so.—Has the Colonel definitely said he would be here?

THE CAPTAIN: *(Gets up.)* Well—that is, he wants to come unexpectedly, as a surprise, as they say. . . . I'm waiting for word from him by telegraph any minute—any minute. . . . *(He goes out, left.)* I'll be back momentarily.

119

ALICE: There you have your man! Would you call him human?

KURT: The last time you asked me that question, I answered "no." But now I believe he is typical of the common-place creatures who have taken possession of the earth. . . . Perhaps even we belong in that category of people who use others and take advantage of every opportunity from which they can benefit.

ALICE: He has eaten you and yours alive—and still you defend him?

KURT: I have suffered worse things.—But this man-eater has left my soul untouched; it was more than he could swallow.

ALICE: What have you encountered that could have been worse?

KURT: You ask me that?

ALICE: Do you mean to be rude?

KURT: No, I don't wish to be, and therefore—don't ask me again.

THE CAPTAIN: *(Enters from the left.)* The telegram was there waiting for me.—Will you read it to me, Alice, it's difficult for me to see. *(He seats himself haughtily in the easy chair.)* Read it!—Kurt can stay! . . .

> *(Alice reads the telegram hastily to herself, and shows consternation.)*

THE CAPTAIN: We-ell? Doesn't it please you, eh? *(Alice is silent and regards the Captain fixedly. The Captain, sarcastically.)* From whom is it?

ALICE: It's from the Colonel.

THE CAPTAIN: *(Self-satisfied.)* That's what I imagined. What does the Colonel say?

ALICE: This is what he says: "Because of Miss Judith's impertinent telephone message, I consider the relationship terminated for ever."

> *(She eyes the Captain fixedly.)*

THE CAPTAIN: Read it again—if you please.

ALICE: *(Reads speedily.)* "Because of Miss Judith's impertinent telephone message, I consider the relationship terminated—for ever."

THE CAPTAIN: *(Pales.)* This is just like Judith!

ALICE: And you—you are Holofernes.

THE CAPTAIN: What are you, then?

ALICE: You'll know soon enough!

THE CAPTAIN: *(In a rage.)* This is you handiwork!

ALICE: No. *(The Captain attempts to get up and unsheath his sabre, but collapses in his chair from a stroke of apoplexy.)* Now you have what you deserve!

THE CAPTAIN: *(Whimpering like a very old man.)* Don't be angry with me—I am so sick. . . .

ALICE: Are you? I am glad you are!

KURT: Let us take him out and put him to bed.

ALICE: No—I don't want to touch him.
(She rings.)

THE CAPTAIN: *(As before.)* Don't be angry with me! *(To Kurt.)* Look after my children.

KURT: This is precious. He wants me to look after his children after having stolen mine from me.

ALICE: Self-deceiving, as ever.

THE CAPTAIN: Look after my children!
(He continues stammering and mumbling incoherent blah-blah-blahs.)

ALICE: At last that tongue of his has been curbed.—Now he can no longer lie, or boast, or wound.—You, Kurt, who believe in a God, thank Him on my behalf—thank Him for setting me free from my imprisonment—from the wolf—from the vampire!

KURT: Don't, don't, Alice!

ALICE: *(Close to the Captain, in his face.)* Where is that strength of yours—your *own* strength—now? Where is it? And your energy? *(The Captain, speechless, spits in her face.)* So you can still spit venom, you viper, can you? Then I'll tear out your tongue! *(She slaps him in the face.)* His head is off, but still he blushes!—Oh, Judith! You marvelous, adorable girl whom I have borne, like my vengeance, under my heart. It is you who have set us all free!—If you have more than one head, you Hydra, we'll take them, too. *(She pulls his beard.)*

121

Oh, to think that justice still exists on earth! There were times when I thought there might be—but I never quite believed it. Ask God to forgive me for doubting, Kurt. Yes, there *is* a justice! And now *I*, too, join the sheep. Tell Him that, Kurt! The merest taste of good fortune tends to make us better, but when we meet with nothing but adversity, we all turn into wolves. . . . *(The Lieutenant enters, rear.)* The Captain has suffered a stroke, Lieutenant. Will you help us, please, to roll the chair into the next room?

THE LIEUTENANT: Madam. . . .

ALICE: What is it?

THE LIEUTENANT: Why. . . . Miss Judith. . . .

ALICE: Help us with this first—then you can tell me about Miss Judith. *(The Lieutenant and Kurt roll out the chair, left.)* Out with the cadaver! Out with it! And open the doors and windows wide—so that this room will be aired out! *(She throws open the French windows, rear. The weather has now cleared.)* Phew!

KURT: Are you going to desert him now?

ALICE: When a ship has foundered, the crew abandons it and saves itself. I don't see why I should lay out a decaying animal! Let the dissecting-room or the morgue take care of him! A flower-bed would be too good for such a wheelbarrowful of foulness!—Now I am going to bathe so that I may rid myself of all this filth and nastiness—if I can ever cleanse it away?

> *(Judith, hatless, is seen on the balustrade outside. She is waving a handkerchief to someone out at sea.)*

KURT: *(Calling in the direction of the French windows.)* Who is out there? Judith! *(Calls again.)* Judith!

JUDITH: *(Enters, cries aloud:)* He is gone!

KURT: Who?

JUDITH: Allan—he is gone!

KURT: Without saying good-bye?

JUDITH: He said good-bye to me, and sends his love to you, Uncle.

ALICE: Oh, so this is what. . . .

JUDITH: *(Throwing herself into Kurt's arms.)* He is gone!

KURT: He will be back, my dear child!

ALICE: Or we shall go where he is.

KURT: *(With a gesture toward the door on the left.)* And leave Edgar! What would people . . .

ALICE: People! Bah!—Judith, come and embrace me! *(Judith goes to Alice, who kisses her on the forehead.)* Would you like to go to Allan?

JUDITH: How can you ask, Mother?

ALICE: But your father has been stricken. . . .

JUDITH: Why should I care—after what he has done?

ALICE: That's my Judith!—Oh, I love you, Judith!

JUDITH: Besides, Father is not small in anything he does—and he dislikes sickly sentimentality. You may say what you like, but Father certainly has a personality and style about him!

ALICE: Yes—of a certain kind.

JUDITH: But I imagine he has no great longing to see me after the telephone call I made to the Colonel!—Well, he should never have tried to marry me off to that old fogy! No, Allan —Allan is for me! *(She throws herself into the arms of Kurt.)* I'm aching to go to Allan!

   (She tears herself from Kurt and runs outside, waving her handkerchief. Kurt hastens after her and waves also.)

ALICE: To think that a flower can sprout and grow out of filth and foulness! *(The Lieutenant enters from the left.)* Well?

THE LIEUTENANT: Oh, Miss Judith. . . .

ALICE: Do you find Judith's name so enchanting that you have to coo it, and forget the man who is dying?

THE LIEUTENANT: Yes, but she said. . . .

ALICE: She? Speak her name instead, then.—But tell me first— how is he now—in there?

THE LIEUTENANT: It is all over. . . .

ALICE: All over?—Oh God, I thank you—for myself, and for all others—thank you for having delivered us from this evil!— Let me take your arm, Lieutenant! I want to go out—out to

123

breathe—to breathe! (*The Lieutenant offers her his arms. Alice stops abruptly.*) Did he say anything before the end came?

THE LIEUTENANT: Yes. He said a few words.

ALICE: What did he say?

THE LIEUTENANT: He said: "Father forgive them, for they know not what they do!"

ALICE: I do not understand. . . .

THE LIEUTENANT: Yes, Miss Judith's father was a good man, a noble man. . . .

ALICE: (*Calls.*) Kurt! (*Kurt comes in.*) It is all over!

KURT: Oh!

ALICE: Do you know what his last words were? No, you couldn't guess. . . . "Forgive them, for they know not what they do."

KURT: How would you interpret that?

ALICE: I assume he meant that *he* had always done what is righteous and died as a man who had been wronged by life.

KURT: He will be given a beautiful funeral oration, no doubt.

ALICE: And plenty of wreaths—from the non-commissioned officers.

KURT: Yes.

ALICE: About a year ago I heard him say: "It seems to me that life is a hoax."

KURT: Are you suggesting that, even in death, he is the buffoon, jeering at us?

ALICE: No. But now that he is dead, I suddenly feel a strange inclination to speak well of him.

KURT: Yes, let us do that.

THE LIEUTENANT: Miss Judith's father was a good and a noble man!

ALICE: (*To Kurt.*) There you hear!

KURT: "They know not what they do." How many times did I not ask whether he knew what he was doing? And you thought he didn't know. Let us therefore forgive him!

ALICE: Riddles! Riddles!—But now we have peace in the house —the awesome peace of death . . . awesome as that solemn and profound anxiety which prevails when a child is about to be born. I can hear the silence—can see on the floor the impression made by the easy-chair in which he was wheeled away. . . . And I have a feeling that my own life has now come to an end, that I am on the road to decay and dissolution! It is very strange, but do you know that these plain words uttered by the Lieutenant—and he is a simple-hearted, unsophisticated young man—they still ring in my ears. . . . And now they have become a weight on my soul. . . . My husband—the love of my youth. . . . Yes, you may laugh— but he *was*, in spite of everything, a good and noble man.

KURT: In spite of everything? Yes, and he did have courage— the way he fought for his existence, and his family's!

ALICE: Think of all the vexations and worries he had, the humiliations—all of which he erased, obliterated, so that he could continue and go on—and on!

KURT: He was a frustrated, defeated man—a man passed by! That is the sum total of it!—Alice—go to him—go inside!

ALICE: No—I can't. . . . While we were speaking, the image of him in his youth has come back to me. . . . I saw him—I see him now before me—see him as he was at the age of twenty. . . . I must have loved that man—once!

KURT: And—hated him!

ALICE: *And*—hated him!—May peace be with him!
       (*She walks toward the door on the left. There she stops, her hands clasped.*)

END OF PART II

125

BY AUGUST STRINDBERG

IN THE NORTON LIBRARY

The Dance of Death (Paulson, tr.)
"A Dream Play" and Four Chamber Plays (Stormy Weather, The House that Burned, The Ghost Sonata, The Pelican) (Johnson, tr.)
Pre-Inferno Plays (The Father, Lady Julie, Creditors, The Stronger, The Bond) (Johnson, tr.)

IN LIVERIGHT PAPERBACK

The Natives of Hemso (a novel) (Paulson, tr.)